Customer Once, Client Forever

Customer Once, Client Forever

12 Tools for Building Lifetime Business Relationships

RICHARD BUCKINGHAM

Foreword By Paul B. Brown, co-author of *Customers for Life*

KIPLINGER BOOKS
Washington, D.C.

Published by
The Kiplinger Washington Editors, Inc.
1729 H Street, N.W.
Washington, DC 20006

Library of Congress Cataloging-in-Publication Data

Buckingham, Richard, 1963-
Customer once, client forever : 12 tools for building lifetime business relationships / Richard Buckingham.
p. cm.
Includes bibliographical references and index.
ISBN 0-938721-82-8 (alk. paper)
1. Customer services--United States. 2. Consumer satisfaction--United States.
I. Title.

HF5415.5 .B799 2001
658.8'12--dc21 00-047823

This publication is intended to provide guidance in regard to the subject matter covered. It is sold with the understanding that the author and publisher are not herein engaged in rendering legal, accounting, tax or other professional services. If such services are required, professional assistance should be sought.

First edition. Printed in the United States of America.
9 8 7 6 5 4 3 2 1

Kiplinger publishes books and videos on a wide variety of personal-finance and business-management subjects. Check our Web site (www.kiplinger.com) for a complete list of titles, additional information and excerpts. Or write:

Cindy Greene
Kiplinger Books & Tapes
1729 H Street, N.W.
Washington, DC 20006
e-mail: cgreene@kiplinger.com

To order, call 800-280-7165; for information about volume discounts, call 202-887-6431.

Dedication

This book is dedicated with respect and gratitude to my clients who have allowed me the opportunity to serve them.

And a special dedication to my father, John D. Buckingham, and everyone else I had the opportunity to work with at Sun Control Systems. My father taught me the importance of having a healthy respect for your clients. I could never have written this book without the experience of working at Sun Control. Thank you.

Acknowledgments

I am indebted to many people for their advice and assistance throughout the development of this book:

To all the people in my workshops who over the past seven years, either by filling out the feedback forms or asking questions, continually improved the quality of the material.

To my clients and associates who took the time to read and comment on earlier manuscripts. I am especially grateful to Randy Shackelford, Frank Bloom, Susan Matthews, Brent Kynoch and my brother Dan Buckingham. Their input has made this a much better book.

To Kent Slepicka. Kent's level judgment, intellect and good humor were instrumental in completing this book. In addition, I'm grateful to Kent for his many suggestions in polishing the GoalStar margin, call-out notes.

To Paul B. Brown, co-author of *Customers for Life,* for his guidance and suggestions. *Customers for Life* is the best business book I have ever read. Buy it and read it.

To everyone at Kiplinger, all of whom have been a pleasure to work with:

To Knight Kiplinger, who took my telephone request for a referral to a literary agent and referred me instead to Kiplinger Books. Because of his interest, *Customer Once, Client Forever* is the Kiplinger Book that you are now holding.

To David Harrison, who strikes that perfect balance of getting things done and being a pleasure to work with. Thanks also to Pat Esswein, who I admire for her desire to always find that exact word to properly convey an idea.

Lastly, thanks to Rosemary Neff, who copyedited and proofed the book, and to Heather Waugh who designed the book and put together a winning and inviting cover design.

To the many outstanding teachers in my life, especially Ed Sundt, Charles Wortman and Keith Saylor. All three taught me that how you arrive at an answer is as important as the answer itself. They taught me to think.

To my mother, Betty Buckingham, because everything in this book is second nature to her.

Finally, to my family and friends, then and now, who supported and encouraged me during this endeavor.

Richard Buckingham
January 2001
Bethesda, Maryland

Table of Contents

Foreword

While Carl Sewell and I would like to think our collective good looks had something to do with the fact that our book, *Customers for Life,* has now sold close to a million copies, the truth is a lot less prosaic. People are hungry for ways to learn how to turn good customer service into a *business strategy.*

This is something that Richard D. Buckingham understands. In the summer of 1997, Rick contacted me about a book he was writing. He said he wanted to help his clients—and others—convert one-time buyers into lifetime clients. Over the past two years, I have watched a book develop.

Drawing on his own experiences, as well as the examples of others such as Sam Walton and Johnson & Johnson, Rick presents a simple, straightforward strategy for increasing sales—and profits. Both his approach and his recommendations are timeless. *Customer Once, Client Forever* is a welcome addition to the ongoing effort of improving the dialogue between companies and their clients.

Business is as competitive as it has ever been. You must do all you can to keep your clients for life. Reading this book is an excellent place to begin.

PAUL B. BROWN
Co-author, *Customers for Life*
Cape Cod Bay, Massachusetts

Introduction

Several times each year, my assistant will buzz my intercom and tell me there's someone on the phone who is very upset and insists on talking with "Mr. Kiplinger." She has already offered, very courteously, to help him with his problem or refer him to someone who can, but he is adamant about talking to "the man at the top."

So what do I do? Ask my assistant to tell the caller I'm in a meeting or out of town? No, I take the call...just as my grandfather took such calls decades ago, and just as my father and I have done for many years. And if the person happened to write me, rather than call, I write him back, with a personal letter.

There are probably plenty of corporate CEOs who feel that spending a few minutes on the phone with aggrieved customers is beneath them, or a distraction from their more important duties. But at the Kiplinger publishing organization, we've never felt that way. To us, our subscribers—whom we consider to be clients, rather than merely customers—are the most important people in our world. If I don't have time to talk with them—whenever they call, for whatever reason—whom should I have time for?

So I take these calls. The caller might be upset about our mishandling of his subscription renewal, or he might be angry about something we wrote in one of our periodicals—something he considers to be inaccurate, unfair or injurious to his business.

The first thing I say is, "How can I help you?" and then I listen. The caller is often so surprised to be talking with "the man at the top," and so surprised that I am really interested in his problem, that he calms down immediately. If our company made a mistake, I apologize at once, no excuses, and offer to make restitution, by extending his subscription at no extra charge or sending him a gift copy of one of our books. If it's an editorial issue on which I can't make amends, I thank him for his opinion and tell him that, while I may not agree, I respect his point of view. If the caller seems inclined to talk a bit longer, I ask him what field he is in, how his business is doing, and what new trends and challenges he's facing. By the end of the talk, after I've thanked him for his patronage, we usually part as friends.

These conversations sometimes take 10 or 15 minutes—all for a subscriber who might add as little as $20, $60 or $80 a year to our revenue, depending on which of our publications he takes. So is this a waste of my time? Hardly.

You see, a publishing business is a prototype of the "lifetime client" relationship that Rick Buckingham is talking about in this wonderful new book, *Customer Once, Client Forever.* Publications succeed or fail on their ability to renew their subscribers year after year, and this, in turn, is dependent on serving their readers' needs—producing the information they want, delivering it fast, and straightening out the problems that occasionally arise, with courtesy and efficiency.

Our company has survived and thrived for more than 80 years because our publications have high subscription renewal rates—much higher than similar periodicals. And we have high renewal rates because we are fanatical about serving our subscribers' needs in any way we can.

As Mr. Buckingham points out throughout this book, great customer service doesn't mean you talk to your clients only when there's a problem—quite the opposite. It requires regularly keeping in touch with them—to inquire about their needs, to anticipate their concerns and to find out how you can serve them better.

Mr. Buckingham makes an astute point when he urges businesses to "under-promise and over-deliver," surprising their clients with service that doesn't just meet, but exceeds, their expectations. This is a lesson that we at Kiplinger took to heart many years ago. Since our founding in 1920, we've been an information service to our subscribers, not just a publisher. Every subscription, however modestly priced, carries with it the privilege of asking our editors for customized information and judgment on any subject we write about: "What's the outlook for natural-gas prices next year?" Or "Will that new OSHA rule be enacted or postponed?" Or "How can I get some information on trade with Ecuador?"

Relatively few of our subscribers take us up on this offer in any given week, but when they do, we respond to their query with speed and accuracy—and the client is surprised and impressed. We think this surprising level of personal service is reflected in our renewal rates, and we hope the client tells a few friends that "Kiplinger was there for me when I needed help."

Is this an expensive way for us to do business? Sure it is. But retaining loyal clients with top-notch service is ultimately less expensive—and much more profitable in the long run—than having to replace disgruntled customers.

That message is at the heart of Mr. Buckingham's new book. He is a master salesman who discovered, by trial and error, that business success depends not only on offering a quality product at a fair price but also on delivering that product with superb service before, during and after the sale. His book is a readable, entertaining sales-and-service bible for everyone in business, from the sales staff and customer-service phone operators to the highest levels of senior management. Extending that old adage, "In successful companies, everyone sells," Mr. Buckingham would add, "Everyone is in client service."

Mr. Buckingham is a sought-after consultant and trainer for businesses large and small. In his seminars and in this book, he makes rich use of colorful and thoughtful anecdotes about the best—and worst—practices he has observed in the businesses that he has served or patronized as a customer.

There is nothing magical about the lessons in *Customer Once, Client Forever.* They are based, above all, on principles of square-dealing, fair play and treating your clients the way you wish to be treated when you're the customer. But surprisingly often, many businesses either never take the trouble to learn these lessons or forget them in the frantic press of their daily grind. And, as Mr. Buckingham points out repeatedly, the most successful, client-friendly businesses never rest on their laurels. They constantly renew their commitment to client service with regular self-assessment, employee training and benchmarking of their business practices.

I learned—and relearned—a lot of valuable lessons from this book, and I'm sure you will, too.

From all of us at the Kiplinger organization, our best wishes to you and your colleagues for success in developing your own loyal corps of "clients forever."

Knight A. Kiplinger
Editor in Chief
The Kiplinger Letter,
Kiplinger's Personal Finance magazine
and Kiplingerforecasts.com
Washington, D.C.

How to Maximize Your Use of This Book

Having read many business books myself and noticed their lack of user-friendliness, I developed six features to make *Customer Once, Client Forever* as useful as possible to my readers.

Read the notes in the margin for key ideas and quick reference.

THE 12 LIFETIME TOOLS. To give the book structure, make it easy to understand and make the strategies easy to apply, I've designed each Lifetime Tool to build on the one before it. Read the Table of Contents first to get an overview of the book and see exactly where we are headed. It's best to read each chapter in sequence. The goal of this book is to offer a comprehensive business philosophy.

THE GOALSTAR SIDE NOTES IN THE MARGIN. To draw out the main nuggets of wisdom and allow for quick reference, I've developed the GoalStar margin notes (named for my business). These margin notes contain the key strategies of the chapter; they are the *Reader's Digest* version of the book. With few exceptions, the margin notes refer to material on the same page or the adjacent one. I've designed this feature for the seasoned business veteran who wants to get a quick summary of the book's high points. It takes about 30 minutes to read all the margin notes.

In addition, the margin space allows room for

you to take notes. Use a highlighter and note key ideas. If you take the time to note them, you will more probably apply the principle today, tomorrow, next week, next month and next year. You will find great success with everyday awareness and application of these strategies.

TRUE STORIES. We all learn best through stories. To illustrate key strategies, each Lifetime Tool contains at least one true story to highlight these skills in the real world. All of the true stories are flagged with a headline that begins with the words "True Story." No matter what the nature or degree of your business experience, you can read just the true stories and gain many valuable business strategies.

QUESTIONS FOR YOU. The strategies in this book are of little use unless you apply them. To remind you that to be successful you must apply what you have read, each chapter includes specific questions addressed to you, the reader. They're highlighted with a headline that reads "Questions for You." You will gain more from this book by answering these questions. It's not what I write that matters; it's what you do with what I write.

THINGS TO DO "MONDAY MORNING." To give you action steps that are easy to implement, I developed "Things to Do Monday Morning," suggestions that end each chapter. Read and implement daily these action steps. If you find these suggestions particularly helpful, cut them out or photocopy them for your immediate reference.

THE READER SURVEY. To continually improve the quality of this book, I've included a reader survey (the GoalStar Continual Improvement Survey) to gain your input. The reader survey is located on pages 281-282. It's a good idea to read the survey questions before you read the book. As you read, think about and answer the survey questions. Also you will find a blank survey form on my Web site at www.goalstar.com.

In summary, if you are new in business, read the book cover to cover. If you are a seasoned veteran, read the GoalStar margin notes, the true stories and the questions posed to the reader. If you desire further explanation, read the entire text.

I recommend you reread this book every year. These strategies are timeless. No matter where you think you are in your career, they will allow you to better serve your clients and take your business to a higher level.

After you finish this book, please complete the reader survey and mail, fax or e-mail it to me. If you like this book, pass it along to a business associate. In addition, feel free to call or e-mail any additional comments to my office. I appreciate all your input.

Customer Once, Client Forever

Understanding the Philosophy of Lifetime Clients

THE PHILOSOPHY

CUSTOMER ONCE, CLIENT FOREVER

In this introduction, I'll share:

- **Why they are clients and not customers**
- **The definition of a lifetime client**
- **Seven compelling reasons to develop lifetime clients**

This book contains a very simple premise. The closer you are to your clients, the more successful you will be in business. The stronger your client relationship, the more profitable you will be. It's just that simple. Every single chapter of this book is dedicated to building the strongest lifetime client partnership possible.

I've been in the business world for 20 years. When I first started in business, I found minimal joy and satisfaction in my work. Although I worked hard, I didn't seem to enjoy what I was doing. I often saw brief successes turn into missed opportunities, as clients would wander off to one of my competitors.

I had never really considered the value of having clients for life, nor had I developed any specific strategies for keeping clients for life. Although I have a good education, I didn't know what individual steps I could take to win lifetime client relationships—or even that that should be my goal. I stumbled along making a sale here and there but seemed to start every business day at square one, looking for new clients.

Then I began to ask myself: "If I'm going to take my time and energy to satisfy clients, why not keep them for life?" Once I realized that my goal should be to keep clients for life rather than to make a one-time sale, I began focusing more and more on serving my clients and building long-term business relationships. I made some missteps early on but learned from them, always focusing on achieving those lifetime relationships that I now realize were key to my success.

Getting and keeping clients became easier. I developed one strategy, then another, and began putting them together into a set of strategies—Lifetime Tools for Lifetime Clients. I found my strategies worked best when I began applying them methodically. My business life became richer and more successful. Success bred success, as the satisfaction I felt in succeeding drove me to seek even better ways to attract and keep clients.

First you must decide you want lifetime clients.

As I worked hard to develop business, I gained greater respect for my customers. I started to call them clients. For me, "customers" are those who buy a product or service one time and don't return. I found I didn't have the proper concern or respect for a customer.

The word "client," however, implies an ongoing relationship. Such relationships are built on trust and respect. In a nutshell, I learned that "customer" implied a transaction; "client" implied a long-term relationship. You should want the lifetime client relationship. After all, no matter what industry you work in, clients ultimately pay your salary.

As I mentioned, one of the reasons my early days were so difficult was that I didn't know where to turn for good information on developing and maintaining clients. Many books presented various business strategies, but none had a clearly defined method for building lifetime client relationships. Most of the current "sales training" guides on the market merely rehash the same material—"prospect, suspect," "cat, mouse," "guerrilla marketing," "they say, you say." I know because I've read them.

Few books offer the complete picture, including all the specifics of how to build a lifetime relationship with a client. In *Customer Once, Client Forever,* I fill that void.

These strategies are not esoteric; they're based on common sense. However, sometimes what's right in front of you—what seems most obvious—is hardest to see. And although you may stumble onto specific strategies that work, as I did in my early years of business, realizing how they interrelate—how to develop an effective process you can follow—may prove elusive. That's what this book is—a comprehensive and systematic process you can follow, using a simple set of strategies, to develop lifetime clients.

You can call them customers, but treat them as clients.

The tools in this book will help you succeed not just in your business relationships but in all your relationships. They're based on one fundamental principle: To achieve success in relationships, you must focus on what you can do for the other person rather than what that person can do for you.

Winning clients for life is all about service. When you serve your clients well, financial success follows. More important, serving your clients well brings you greater satisfaction in your work. While my paycheck grew steadily as I applied these tools, it was the satisfaction in my work that truly inspired me. I hope that is what you find when you start to use the tools in this guide.

Much as sailors chart their course with buoys, you can chart your course in business with the markers I'll give you in this guide. As you follow the course I've laid out for you, applying these strategies methodically and consistently, you will succeed. While the lessons in this guide are simple, their application will be challenging. I urge you to read and reread this guide and to implement all the suggestions. When you succeed in building client relationships, recognize and note which suggestions aided you. When you encounter a temporary setback, notice which ones you didn't apply and apply them at the next opportunity.

If you're not convinced you want clients for life, keep reading. I will explain the value of keeping clients for life and the cost of losing them. Once you've completed this introduction, you should be ready to learn my strategies for keeping clients for life. Each tool builds on the previous one to give you an integrated, step-by-step method for developing lifetime client relationships.

Lifetime clients will consider you their trusted adviser and will refer others to you.

I include true stories because I believe, as I mentioned earlier, we all learn best through real-life examples. I also include a list of resources in the Appendix (pages 263-272) I've found helpful in developing the Lifetime Tools. After you complete this book, I suggest you buy and read two or three of the books in the resource list.

This guide is written for everyone in business who wants to develop and maintain lifetime clients—from the aspiring new salesperson to seasoned CEOs who want to take their firm to the next level.

Read the guide, apply the strategies, and you will start to build lifetime relationships with your clients and find greater fulfillment in your work.

Defining a Lifetime Client

At the outset, let's clearly define what a lifetime client is. Lifetime clients are those who are so pleased with your product and service that they come back to you after the initial sale, repeatedly, for a business lifetime (ten years, according to the industry standard). Clients do this because they trust and rely on you. You become their trusted adviser. They call you first and prefer to use you instead of anyone else.

In addition to returning themselves—and here is the real benefit—lifetime clients refer others to you with only their highest recommendations. Referral clients are sold on you before they even hear your voice.

Referral clients are already sold, before they even call you.

Your ultimate business goal is to have clients singing your praises at business lunches, on the golf course and at social events. You can see only so many clients during the course of a day: You want your existing clients to be so pleased with you that they send you business. Your existing clients in effect become your sales force.

Is everyone a potential lifetime client? That's up to you and depends on your particular business. I have reached success by being inclusive rather than exclusive. How will you ever know if the client you elect not to serve would have had a large transaction or a nice referral for you? To completely illustrate the potential of a lifetime client, let me share a true story.

TRUE STORY: The Jeweler Who Didn't See the Value in Lifetime Clients

I recently purchased a pair of pearl earrings as a present. On the recommendation of a good friend, I called a local jeweler and inquired about prices. The jeweler told me his pearl earrings ran anywhere from $75 to $1,000. I went to the store figuring I would purchase a nice pair for around $300. No such luck. The next least expensive pair after the $75 pair was $500, which was more than I wanted to spend.

Since I was already at the store and needed to get the present that day, I decided to buy the $500 pair. After all, the jeweler came highly recommended, and the earrings were beautiful.

Your clients should become your unpaid sales force.

The person who received the earrings noticed a slight blemish on one of the earrings that I didn't notice when I purchased them. She was also surprised that such nice earrings did not have screw backs, which are more secure than other fastenings.

So I returned to the jeweler slightly miffed, pointed out the blemish and asked for screw backs. He put on the screw backs and replaced the blemished pearl. I had to make a third trip back to the jeweler to pick up the earrings.

A couple of months later, my friend was taking her earrings off when one of the pearls fell off the earring and into her hand. She was relieved that she had caught the pearl but upset that it had come loose. The week before, she had been out on the water. Had the pearl dropped out then, it could easily have fallen overboard and she never would have found it.

Now I took my fourth trip to the jeweler. The store was on the third-floor corner of a busy shopping mall. Parking nearby was next to impossible. I had to park in the basement and go up four or five flights of stairs, depending on what level I was lucky enough to get in the parking garage. In short, this was not an easy store to reach.

At this point, I was also beginning to wonder if I hadn't been taken advantage of in terms of the price. As I mentioned, $500 was more than I had wanted to spend, and within the three months since I'd bought them, all I'd had were problems with the earrings.

I was a little upset by this time. When I politely expressed my dismay first with a blemished earring and now with a broken one, the jeweler casually replied, "Oh, that happens." Oh, that happens? I went from being a little upset to being outright angry.

Don't just sell; build lifetime client relationships.

The jeweler never apologized, which surprised me. I asked if I could wait while he fixed the earring and he said that the man who did that type of work was not in. I could come back later in the day and pick it up. This was the Friday morning of a busy holiday weekend. The very last thing I wanted to do was to head back into Washington, D.C., at rush hour to pick up something that should have been correct in the first place. I would rather have had a root canal!

At this point I was so disgusted with the situation that I decided to have the pearl repaired at another store. I have four jewelers within walking distance of my office. When I got back to my office, I took the earrings to all four. Rather than tell me, "Oh, that happens," these jewelers told me two very important facts about these particular earrings: the cups (the portion that held the pearls) were too small, and the stems that went into the pearls were too short.

The pearls were improperly mounted. Given that fact, no matter how often they were glued, the pearls could fall out again. I ended up paying an additional $85 to have the pearls properly mounted, something that should have been done when the earrings were made.

What baffles me was that the jeweler I bought the earrings from did not meet and exceed my needs. If he had, my lifetime purchases with him would have far overweighed any additional money he would have spent taking care of me. In addition to making lifetime purchases, I also would have referred business to him.

To get a better understanding of the philosophy of lifetime clients, let's look at the potential business the jeweler missed. Noting that Washington, D.C., jewelry prices are somewhat inflated, let's look at some estimates of future sales:

Don't cold-call. Do outstanding work and clients will seek you out.

- **When I purchased the earrings,** I told the jeweler the next present would be a pearl necklace. At that time, I inquired what a nice strand of pearls cost. Estimated cost: $1,500 to $3,000.
- **I think I will get engaged at some point,** and at that time, I'll want to buy an appropriate diamond engagement ring for my fiancée. Estimated cost: $8,000 and up.
- **What goes well with a diamond ring?** Diamond stud earrings. Estimated cost: $3,000 and up.
- **When I get married,** I will need two wedding bands. Estimated cost: $5,000.

The jeweler lost at least $19,000 in future business—and that is a conservative estimate—not to mention all the business I might have referred his way. Don't forget I was referred to him and the jeweler knew that. Not only did he lose my business, he lost the business of the person that referred me. That's maybe another $19,000.

Just as he would have gained economically with a lifetime relationship, I would have gained from developing a lifetime relationship with a jeweler I could trust. The last thing I wanted to do was search for a new source of jewelry. However, because of the original jeweler's poor service, I had to develop a new source.

To develop a lifetime client, the jeweler should have done the following:

- **Properly explained the pricing of the earrings** on my first telephone inquiry. "We have a pair at $75 and the next pair is $500."
- **Mounted the earrings properly** before he put them in the display case.
- **Sold only unblemished pearls.**
- **Apologized profusely for the inconvenience** he caused with the blemish and the improper mountings.
- **Acknowledged and empathized with my feelings,** and fixed the earrings properly the very first time.
- **Had someone there to repair the earrings on the spot** or, perhaps better yet, offered to have them couriered to me later that day (at his expense), and again apologized for all the inconvenience he had caused. Maybe at that point he could have inquired about when I would purchase that pearl necklace.
- **Developed enough rapport and trust that he could have learned what was wrong with his pearls,** so he could prevent a future mishap and the possibility of losing another lifetime client. He lost not only me but my friend as well. How much other business will he lose?

Spend less time prospecting and more time properly processing existing client transactions.

He had the opportunity at each of these steps—or, better stated, missteps—to win me back. But he missed every opportunity. I offered him numerous chances to do the right thing, and I would have been his lifetime client if he had cooperated.

The jeweler in this story obviously didn't understand the value of a lifetime client. Even if he had, would he have known to take the actions I describe—which are based on the strategies I offer in this guide?

QUESTIONS FOR YOU

- *Do you appreciate the value of lifetime clients?*
- *Do you have the proper strategies to keep your clients for life?*

Returning clients bring you greater profitability.

Profitability Is in the Lifetime Relationship

What the jeweler didn't see, and what I missed in my early business transactions, was that profitability is in the lifetime client relationship. You may not make money on the first or second client transaction. You will make money on the third, fourth and fifth sales and on all the referral business clients send you. If the jeweler had properly served my needs, he would have had at least $19,000 of future business. (In Lifetime Tool 11, I'll show you how to determine the dollar value of a lifetime client using the GoalStar Lifetime Client Model.)

Are you keeping your clients for life? Are you earning maximum profitability with your clients? You may be new to business and trying to figure out how to close that first sale. What will you do once you make that sale—start all over again with another new buyer?

You may be a seasoned veteran with a solid track record. But are your clients returning, giving you all their return business and referring other prospective clients to you?

Let's share some compelling reasons to keep clients for life.

Seven Compelling Reasons to Keep Clients for Life

You have made a significant investment of money and time in reading this book. I want to show you exactly what you will gain when you turn one-time buyers into lifetime clients. Here are seven reasons to convert one-time buyers into lifetime clients:

You don't want to chase clients; you want clients to chase you.

1. **You don't have to search for new clients.**
2. **Your sales increase.**
3. **Your market position strengthens.**
4. **Your clients' loyalty increases.**
5. **Your costs of doing business decrease.**
6. **Your profits increase.**
7. **You find greater joy and satisfaction in your daily work.**

1. You Don't Have to Search for New Clients

Why search for new clients when you have plenty of clients right in front of you? My life became much easier once I no longer had to seek out new clients. Rather than my having to search for them, clients found me. My time was leveraged. I could see only so many clients a day. But when I implemented all the strategies I share with you in this book, more clients than I could ever imagine sought me out.

The added benefit of these clients' finding me was that they were more discerning clients. Price was not their main concern. They wanted a fair price, but, more important, they wanted excellent service. I soon began to realize that they wanted a lifetime relationship also.

I found that as I improved my service, not only did the number of prospective clients calling me increase but their commitment to buying from me was much higher—selling became a lot easier! I found that I really enjoyed it. In fact, I soon realized that I was never really selling. I was building lifetime relationships simply by meeting and exceeding clients' needs. My job became a matter of showing up and doing what I was good at. Without realizing it, I had become a trusted adviser to my clients.

When clients seek you out, price is usually not the driving concern.

2. Your Sales Increase

Once I no longer had to seek out new clients, I could concentrate on increasing business with existing clients and the new ones who sought me out. All my clients were serious about doing business. Clients were bringing the business to me. I didn't have to go in search of it. I never had to make cold calls or market my services. Business came from anywhere and everywhere. I spent less and less time prospecting and more and more time closing business and processing client transactions. Because I was more efficient, company profits increased.

In addition, the company's cash flow—the lifeline of all companies—increased. Everyone was happy. The accounting department was happy because money was coming in promptly and regularly. Vendors were happy because they were being paid quickly. The boss was happy because everyone was getting paid. I was happy because I received a paycheck at the end of the week. Over 18 months, the amount of my paychecks doubled and tripled.

3. Your Market Position Strengthens

When I converted one-time buyers into lifetime clients, my company's market position became stronger. When clients were buying from me, they were not buying from the competition. Not only did I improve the company's cash flow, I also boxed out the competition. The gain was exponential. The more market share I captured, the harder it was for the competition to survive, and the more business we ultimately gained.

Complete small transactions well and larger ones will soon follow.

4. Your Clients' Loyalty Increases

Most businesspeople underestimate the value of client loyalty. (We will discuss this further in Lifetime Tools 10 and 11.) They see only the prospect of making a single sale. They see those who walk in their doors *only* as one-time customers and concentrate *only* on making the single sale and the dollars that come with a single transaction. In the long run, one-time buyers will not bring you the highest profits. Profit lies in the repeat and referral business that comes from clients who are loyal to you because you've served them well and earned their trust.

Have you ever received a very small order, completed it successfully, and then a couple of weeks later received a larger order from the same client? It is as if your client sent up a trial balloon to see how it would fare. This happened to me a lot. I took small transactions just as seriously as large transactions because I never knew where they would lead. When I took care of clients and exceeded their expectations, I didn't have to ask for their repeat business. Clients just called again and again. I began to develop pride in my work.

In addition, when I exceeded client expectations, not only would they return but, unbeknownst to me, they referred others. People would just call me, apparently out of the blue, and ask me to become involved in a project.

Most businesspeople fail to recognize the ease of a referral call. By the time prospective clients call, they are 95 percent sold. All you need to do is show up, do what you're good at and close the sale. The prospective client has heard you're good—you just need to confirm it. The referral is the easiest sale you will make outside of repeat business. And best of all, you do not have to spend a cent to gain the sale. Referrals are the reward for doing outstanding business.

Profitability lies in repeat and referral business.

For me, the value of referrals took time to gauge because it took me time to become sharp enough to ask the million-dollar question: "How did you happen to call us?"

If you just get the one-time sale, you are like the gold miner who strikes the top of the vein and leaves with a modest profit. The irony is that the miner neglects the real profit, which is the entire vein. Do not miss the mother lode! Repeat and referral business comes from happy, loyal clients. On pages 240–242, I describe how to estimate the monetary value of a lifetime client on the basis of repeat and referral business.

QUESTION FOR YOU

- *Are you asking your clients how they happened to call you?*

5. Your Costs of Doing Business Decrease

Most companies never take the time to calculate what it costs—in time, effort and money—to develop a client. When I started winning clients for life, I no longer had to spend valuable resources to attract them. *They were coming to me.* I didn't have to put additional wear and tear on my automobile or spend more money on fuel. I avoided wasting time preparing proposals that were never accepted.

My time became more productive because I was dealing with clients who were ready to do business. When I began to look at my time as an investment, my closure rates and sales increased. I took all my projects and transactions more seriously when I realized what it cost me just to get in front of a client. Obvious costs were office overhead, car expenses, entertainment, and association memberships. In addition, there was a hidden cost—that of lost opportunity. Where else could I be investing my time more wisely and effectively? Again, most businesspeople don't put the proper premium on what their time is worth. You will develop more lifetime client relationships when you have a greater awareness of all the costs that are involved.

Compare the higher cost of getting a new client to the lower cost of keeping an existing client.

QUESTION FOR YOU

- *What does it cost you to obtain a lifetime client?*

6. Your Profits Increase

The number of sales you make means nothing if you're not turning a profit. Simply put, profits come from maximizing sales while minimizing costs. Because you are building your business on repeat and referral trade, you are not having to spend money to attract new clients. If you're successful at getting all the benefits listed above, you will turn a profit. If you fail to actualize the potential of lifetime clients, profit will elude you. Remember the story of the jeweler at the beginning of this introduction.

7. You Find Greater Joy and Satisfaction in Your Work

Before seeking new business, seek referrals and repeat business from existing clients.

The real, hidden victory in my developing lifetime client relationships was that, when I turned one-time buyers into lifetime clients, *I found greater joy and satisfaction in my work.* As I mentioned earlier, I felt a sense of pride when someone I had not met before sought me out and not only wanted a bid but wanted to do business with me. For me this was the best reason for turning one-time buyers into lifetime clients.

I began to see that success and long-term profitability did not come just with individual projects or transactions; they came with lifetime relationships with clients. I became more committed to my job. When clients called me and specifically asked for me, I felt great pride.

QUESTION FOR YOU

- *What actions are you taking today to keep your clients for life?*

Recognizing Lifetime Client Opportunities

If you aren't doing so already, I hope you will begin to look at your clients and see three possible business opportunities. When you put this book down and come in contact with your next potential client, either in person, over the telephone or by e-mail, recognize this client represents three opportunities:

1. **Immediate sale or transaction**
2. **Repeat business**
3. **Referral business**

When I was younger and less experienced, I focused only on the immediate sale. As I became more seasoned, I began to recognize that the real opportunity is in the repeat and referral business.

Enter all your clients into a contact-management program. Contact them frequently.

The rest of this book is dedicated to offering the necessary strategies to maximize these client opportunities. For the time being, just recognize the future business opportunities your clients offer you. I like to tell people in workshops that when you are dealing with one client, you are also dealing with 20 potential clients.

How to Turn Satisfied Customers Into Loyal, Lifetime Clients

That's what the rest of this book is about. Now that you see the value of client loyalty, you're ready to start using the tools I've designed to help you build lifetime relationships—the Lifetime Tools. These tools are based on fundamental principles I've learned about winning and keeping clients for life:

- **Cultivate the desire to keep clients for life,** and be willing to continually improve yourself and exceed clients' expectations to win their loyalty.
- **Completely understand your business,** your market and your clients, so you can properly educate your clients.

- **Listen effectively to clients and ask the right questions** to better understand their needs.
- **Make your business run smoothly and efficiently** by systemizing it and thus better serving clients.
- **Ask for clients' and associates' feedback,** and implement their suggestions.
- **Take clients' complaints seriously** by responding swiftly to remedy the situation.
- **Work hard and smart to maintain your current lifetime client relationships** while seeking out new clients to serve.

"Lifetime clients" is a philosophy of conducting business.

In the following chapters, I describe in detail the Lifetime Tools and how to use them. Anyone in any organization can use these tools to win and keep clients for life. No matter whether you're a salesperson, a customer service representative, a manager, a CEO or a receptionist, these tools will help build lifetime client relationships.

THINGS TO DO "MONDAY MORNING"

- **Treat customers like clients.**
- **Close the initial sale** and set yourself up for repeat and referral business.
- **Recognize that the greatest profitability** is in repeat and referral business.

Continually Improving Yourself

LIFETIME TOOL

1

CUSTOMER ONCE, CLIENT FOREVER

In this chapter, I'll share:

- **Why continual improvement is the first step in developing lifetime clients**
- **The three strategies for achieving continual improvement**
- **An example of continual improvement in action**

The single most effective strategy for developing lifetime clients is focusing first on yourself and your skills. No matter how good you think you are, you should always ask yourself, "How can I improve?" "How can I better serve my clients?" The responsibility for doing this rests on you and you alone. To be successful in business, you must be open to learning how to improve. When you ask yourself, before a client has to tell you, how you can improve in business, you are one step ahead of the competition.

Whether you are the CEO of a Fortune 100 company or the new kid on the block, recognize that business is one continual learning experience. If you accept responsibility and are open to learning from your mistakes, you are on your way to success both in business and in life. Be a lifetime student!

TRUE STORY: Baptism by Fire

I am fortunate to have 15 years of solid, hands-on experience in sales, customer service and order fulfillment in the fiercely competitive commercial construction industry. I have yet to find a better environment to learn how to develop and maintain lifetime client relationships. Why?

The construction industry is driven by price and the ability to deliver your product on time.

Most buyers care only about whether you have the lowest price and can do the job correctly and on time. Where you went to school, who you know—none of this matters in the construction business.

You know you've done the best job you can if a buyer wants to continue working with you and tries to renegotiate a bid when your offer is not the lowest. In effect the buyer says, "I'd like to work with you, but you're not offering the lowest price. Give me your best price, and let's see what we can do."

In short, if you can build a lifetime relationship in the construction industry, you can build one in any industry.

Look inward first and ask yourself how you can improve; always be open to suggestions for improvement.

My Three Phases of Continual Improvement

My education about lifetime clients and better business management can be divided into three phases: learning from setbacks, achieving limited success, and finding greater fulfillment.

Phase I: Learning From Setbacks

I had a challenging beginning when I started in business. I was given a telephone and a desk and told to go "sell." I didn't have the opportunity to receive any training. I wasn't smart enough to go to the bookstore, get three or four good business books, and read and absorb all the strategies.

I ventured into the business world unprepared. I had little understanding of the seller-client relationship or its significance in attaining long-term business success. In short, I really didn't understand or appreciate who a client was. I also didn't understand the concept of profitability and was not well versed in the importance and ease of repeat and referral business.

Not surprisingly, I went six months without a significant business transaction. I didn't know where to start to attract or keep clients. I had very little success. The one sale I did make was what was known as a change order—basically a "gimmie," where I did not have to secure the client, but merely give him a price and then proceed with the work. The client sent me a letter and told me to proceed and send him a bill.

Always be reading a good business book. Review the GoalStar reading list in the Appendix.

Even with this simple sale I struggled. Turns out, I left out half of the project cost. What should have been a profitable transaction became a break-even transaction. My frustration was compounded when I recognized that I was not serving anyone, clients or co-workers. I didn't feel good about myself. I wasn't contributing to anyone.

With repeated setbacks slapping me in the face, I finally did start to wise up. I started asking myself, "What am I doing wrong? How can I improve next time?"

I worked with four people who had more experience than I did. I started reaching out and asking for their assistance. I made a point of going to lunch with them and peppering them with questions, such as

- **How do you get clients?**
- **How do you close business?**
- **How do you get clients to call you back?**
- **How would you handle this particular situation?**

I wasn't afraid of suggestions on how to improve. It's amazing how open you can be to suggestions when you're not doing so well. I soon began to see a direct correlation between my openness to learning and my improved performance. I began to develop a set of strategies for achieving success. Within a couple of months, I began to develop an instinct for dealing effectively with issues that used to baffle me. I started closing some business. It wasn't much, but it was business.

You should have a mentor, no matter what stage of your career.

Phase II: Achieving Limited Success

I took all the frustration I was feeling and started to channel it by applying the strategies I'd learned—the same ones I share in this book. Things started to improve. I started to win more and more business, and at a profit, too! I found that success begat success. My list of clients started to grow.

The old adage "be careful what you wish for" comes to mind here. Within 18 months of working in the construction business, I could not control all the incoming telephone calls. Eighteen months before I couldn't get a sale; now I couldn't get any breathing room.

What motivated me to take action and do something about the increasing stress was my realization that, of the 30 calls I was receiving in a day, 28 were checking on the status of existing orders. And my clients were the type who would call back two or three times a morning if I still hadn't produced the answer they were looking for.

I did feel better about myself now that I was bringing in business and serving people. However, my excitement at getting all the new business was rapidly replaced by a sense of being overwhelmed in properly processing the business.

I knew that if I wanted my business to grow, and if I wanted to live a normal life, I had to do something. So I developed and fine-tuned internal systems to process this business. I will explain

these systems in greater detail in Lifetime Tool 8.

Whereas months before I had had little understanding of who a client was, now at least I was in contact with some. However, I still didn't completely understand the importance of having a good relationship with clients or how to build such relationships. I still needed more improvement, to continue to improve my attitude. With some clients, I even had antagonistic relationships—especially those who kept calling and calling. It was the third phase of my development that gave me a more complete and healthy respect for a client.

Clients should call you only once. After that, you should proactively call them.

Phase III: Finding Greater Fulfillment

Since I had achieved positive results in Phase II by channeling my frustrations, asking questions and practicing continual improvement, I used a similar approach in Phase III. I took three important steps:

I took responsibility and became accountable. To be specific, I began to live by the simple credo that clients should have to call me only once. That is, clients would initiate contact and after that I would always proactively call them.

By taking the responsibility for actively contacting clients, not only did I make my life easier by reducing the number of incoming calls, I also made my clients' lives easier. Clients didn't have to track me down. I started to anticipate their needs. The response from my clients was both overwhelming and rewarding. Not only did they return with new transactions sooner, they told friends and associates about me. I did not have to seek out new business. In addition, price became less and less an issue. Service took the forefront.

Second, I raised my standards and expected more of myself. If it took me 30 days to process an order, I set a new standard of 15 days. I still told clients to expect their products in 30 days, but I worked hard to deliver them in 15 days. When I succeeded in delivering in 15 days, I looked like Superman to my clients—not a bad feeling. If I needed extra time, I had that wiggle room with clients.

Anticipate your clients' needs.

I *decided* that I wanted lifetime clients. If I worked hard to serve a client, I wanted all his or her business. Until I focused on wanting that relationship, everything else I did was unimportant. Now I wanted my clients to consider me their trusted adviser. I wanted them to think of me first. I wanted the opportunity to do all their business as well as any referral business they might have.

In short, I found continual improvement was an excellent tool to achieve business success. When I focused on properly serving my existing clients and continuously improving my business systems, my sales skyrocketed and my profitability soared. Business poured in. I didn't have to do a thing except answer the telephone and process orders. Whereas a year and a half earlier I had been chasing business with limited success, now business was chasing me—a rewarding switch.

My job became much more manageable. I didn't feel as hassled and harried as I had before. In fact, I felt better about myself. As I mentioned earlier, I began to find joy and satisfaction with my work. I actually looked forward to coming to work and serving clients' needs.

I now had a much clearer perspective on who a client was. I made the direct correlation that my paycheck came from satisfying and delighting my clients. This entire process taught me to have a deeper and more wholesome respect for my clients. No longer was that telephone call late Friday afternoon or in the middle of lunch an annoyance; it was an opportunity to establish or reinforce the relationship with clients I would keep for life.

Recognize that your clients pay your salary.

By improving and by focusing on *serving* clients, and by using the tools I offer in this book, I began to enjoy the benefits of repeat and referral business and, ultimately, lifetime clients. My clients were happier with the constantly improving service. Work was done sooner and and was done correctly the first time.

In addition, I discovered an added benefit: *My profitability soared.* Because I was improving my service and working more effectively and efficiently, profits increased nicely. I soon realized that it was not the sales volume that ultimately mattered but the amount of profit I made. That's what makes it to the bank.

Lots of business books talk about "sales," but few speak about the importance of profitability. Remember, you are in business to make a profit. Or, as my good friend Craig Schwartz tells his people as they head out for the day, "Sell something at a profit today!"

Three Improvement Strategies

The first lifetime tool for lifetime clients is continual improvement. No matter where you work in an organization—accounting, shipping, technical support or management—you can always improve your performance.

In addition, no matter how much success you've had, you can always improve. Three strategies that will put you on the road to continual improvement today are:

- **Practicing "Liked Best, Next Time" (LB/NT)**
- **Continually improving your attitude**
- **Measuring your performance**

The sooner you analyze your performance, the sooner you will improve.

Practice the "Liked Best, Next Time" Exercise

The best tool I have found to achieve daily continual improvement is "Liked Best, Next Time" (LB/NT; see the worksheet on page 28).

When was the last time you honestly assessed your performance?

Most businesspeople, when they take time to assess their performance (which unfortunately is rare), either give themselves a glowing review without finding a single area of potential improvement or are so hard on themselves that they can't find a single thing they did right.

You will benefit immensely when you develop the skill to evenhandedly and clearly assess your own performance. It will take time to develop this type of awareness, but when you do you will have an outstanding asset that will guarantee future business success.

Every time you don't analyze your performance, you miss a valuable opportunity to learn and grow. LB/NT offers you an excellent opportunity to learn two important things:

1. Recognize specifically what you did well so you can duplicate it in the future. Most of us never take the time to acknowledge properly what we do well and replicate it with other clients.

2. Pinpoint where to improve in the future—something most of us shy away from.

Continual improvement is all about awareness. LB/NT helps you develop a keener awareness of your business performance.

How LB/NT Works

Leverage your talents; improve your shortcomings.

Take any event, positive or negative—a lost sale, a typical sales call, an unhappy customer, a technical mishap, an anniversary of your hire, a production snafu, a new account that you landed, an account that you have temporarily lost, progress toward building a team, anything—and ask yourself two basic questions:

1. **What did I like best about the event?—LB**
2. **What will I do next time to improve?—NT**

Liked Best

Look at the event and notice what went well. Get down to *specific* behaviors. The more specific you are about identifying your actions, the sooner you will improve. For instance, with a sales call, actions to identify might include the following:

- **Developed a good lead**
- **Listened carefully to the client**
- **Asked client good questions**
- **Built rapport with client**
- **Completed proposal quickly, included various options with quote**

Next Time

Applying the principles described above, ask yourself how you will *improve* on your actions next

Use this tool.
It works.

LIKED BEST, NEXT TIME EXERCISE

EVENT ______________________

DATE ______________________

LIKED BEST: What specifically did I do well?

1. ______________________

____

2. ______________________

____

3. ______________________

____

4. ______________________

____

5. ______________________

____

NEXT TIME: How will I improve?

1. ______________________

____

2. ______________________

____

3. ______________________

____

4. ______________________

____

5. ______________________

____

time. Again, get down to specific behaviors. For instance, with a sales call, you might:

- **Ask more directed and pointed questions** to better understand a client's needs
- **Improve rapport** by finding more common ground with client
- **Include recommendation letters** from happy clients in proposal
- **Ask for the business**
- **Ask for the lifetime relationship**
- **Close more strongly by doing a better job of pointing out the client's needs** and stressing your abilities to meet and exceed those needs.

Your greatest challenge is not the competition; it's complacency and mediocrity.

When to Use LB/NT

Use LB/NT whenever you want to improve. If you are a manager, use "Liked Best, Next Time" if you have had an unsuccessful coaching session with an associate. If you are a customer service representative and have just hung up with an unhappy client, do an LB/NT exercise to evaluate that telephone call and the client situation. If you are a salesperson and have lost a sale, take five minutes and analyze your performance so you will win the next sale and the lifetime relationship. Use "Liked Best, Next Time" to measure your overall progress toward developing lifetime clients.

In my office, I have both a thick folder of "Liked Best, Next Time" sheets and an LB/NT computer screen. After every workshop and consulting project, I analyze my performance.

You can use the blank form on the preceding page for the LB/NT exercise. Copy this page so you can use it for future client meetings. Take five minutes now and analyze your last client interaction.

QUESTIONS FOR YOU

- *When was the last time you analyzed your performance?*
- *What did you learn?*
- *How did you improve?*

Suggestions for Optimizing LB/NT

You alone are responsible for your success.

To maximize your use of LB/NT, I have found the following helpful:

Start today. Start an LB/NT folder or an LB/NT template on your computer. If you are in sales, customer service or tech support, take your last three client contacts and analyze them with a written LB/NT exercise.

Look for specific actions you have taken. The more specific the actions you notice, the better your analysis will be. To improve quickly, use a tape recorder to record your telephone conversations with clients. (Make sure you are not violating any laws by this taping.) Analyze your voice tone, your diction, and how you handled the client and situation. You will improve more quickly when you know exactly what you are doing well and where you can improve.

Write your actions down. Rather than berating myself for poor performance, I found success when I channeled my emotions positively and sat down and honestly assessed my performance. You will achieve success faster when you write it down. It heightens your awareness, and that's what makes this exercise work.

Constantly monitor your progress. Read your

LB/NT results often. If you are in sales, read your last LB/NT results before your next appointment. If you are like me, when you start using this exercise, you will have fewer Liked Bests and more Next Times. As you improve, you will see the reverse—more LBs, fewer NTs. Never stop filling out the LB/NT form.

No matter where you think you are in your career, this is an excellent strategy for continual improvement. When you want to go the next level in your business, sharpen your awareness of your performance.

Your actions must match your desire to improve.

Recognize your strengths and see where you can improve. What you see as a weakness may in fact be a strength that you haven't yet learned how to apply effectively. If it truly is a weakness, remember that you can always improve on it.

Learning to recognize your weaknesses and your strengths, and to face your weaknesses head-on, is the only way to grow. Psychologically, when you attack something that you think holds you back, you deflate the issue. What seemed like an insurmountable concern one day will seem laughably easy to resolve after you have faced it. (Don't believe me? At the end of this chapter, I'll share my public-speaking experiences.)

Properly channel your frustrations. Take your frustrations and channel them into doing the LB/NT exercise. Your best bet is to do it immediately after challenging events. That way you'll feel better about yourself because you're doing something constructive rather than dwelling on difficult or unsuccessful events. You're moving forward—developing strategies to avoid such situations again. That's growth.

Rate your performance on a scale of 1 to 10. When you really want to improve, start to assign a rating to your performance. Remember, your goal is to develop a clear, evenhanded assessment of your own performance. Accomplish this by ranking your performance on a scale of 1 to 10: 1 indicates you need the most improvement, 10 says you're excellent.

Before someone else tells you, ask yourself how you can improve.

Never stop learning. Most people are frustrated in their careers because they stop learning and growing. By using "Liked Best, Next Time," you will always be open to growth because you will see where you can improve.

Whether you're improving your strengths or eliminating your weaknesses, the resulting growth is critical to your continuing success. You better serve your clients by continually assessing and improving your own performance. Don't wait for your client, boss or co-worker to tell you how to improve; do it yourself.

Continually Improve Your Attitude—Attitude Is Everything!

The second step toward continual improvement is continually improving your attitude. Most businesspeople underestimate the importance of their attitude. When things go wrong, most businesspeople look everywhere but inward. If they lose a sale or an account, they will blame anyone and anything except themselves. Believe me, I used to do it! It was the client's fault, it was the price, it was the competition, it was the poor market conditions, it was the stock-market drop or it was the rain—anything but me and my performance.

Adopt a Daily Attitude of Self-Assessment

Take responsibility and look inward to see where you can improve. Constantly look for ways to improve the situation and yourself. When you fail to close a sale or when you temporarily lose a client, ask yourself, "What might *I* have done differently to close the sale or retain that account? What is my responsibility?" I found great success when I took more responsibility in my life.

Continual improvement breeds long-term success.

Self-assessment is not easy to undertake. It can be scary. What happens when we find things inside ourselves we don't like, things we should change? Change is something that few of us embrace easily. We like to think we are all right the way we are and don't want to do the work necessary for improvement. Looking outside for the answers is always easier, but you won't find the critical answers, or the success you desire. You usually find only scapegoats.

Whatever reason you may have for avoiding improvement, overcome it. You must adopt an open attitude to learning. This means you must be open to suggestions for improvement—from everyone, including clients. Even more important, this means seeking out feedback when you may not get any. If you are not doing this already, when you complete delivery of your product or service, you need to ask the client, either orally or in written form, "How did I do?" "How can I improve?" We will talk more about this in Lifetime Tool 9, Gaining Valuable Client Feedback. Every time you don't ask a client how you can improve, you miss a valuable opportunity to learn and grow.

For now, initiate a follow-up call to clients to check on the quality of your work. Forming the habit of the post-service follow-up call was one of the most important steps I took in improving my service to clients.

Continual Improvement Is Not Just for Novices

In working with clients, always be willing to learn.

In business, when we enjoy success, we tend to not work as hard as we could or focus on continual improvement as much as we should. One common misconception among businesspeople is that once we have achieved success, we don't need to grow. If I could rectify any one misconception in business, this complacency would be the one. Unless you are learning and growing every day, you are falling backward.

Let me give you an example of this complacency. I have seen many excellent salespeople promoted to managers. While they had stellar sales and people skills, they lacked management and leadership skills. So these excellent salespeople floundered as leaders because they did not look at themselves hard enough and ask two critical questions:

1. **What did I do well?—LB**
2. **How can I improve?—NT**

To compound the situation, these new leaders let ego and ultimately fear get in the way of learning and growing. They didn't need to learn anything, they thought; after all, they had just earned a promotion!

To grow, you must place yourself in challenging situations. Don't be overwhelmed by this. Recognize the tools you have, like "Liked Best, Next Time," and use them.

I suggest that this philosophy and practice of continual improvement is absolutely critical to long-term business success. As you read what Horace Greeley once wrote about an American president, ask yourself: Is this true of you?

"He was open to all impressions and influences and gladly profited by the teaching of events and circumstances, no matter how adverse or unwelcome. There was probably no year of his life that he was not a wiser, cooler and better man than he was the year preceding."

Lest you think attitude is not important in business, let me share with you an example of just how important and profitable a positive attitude in business can be.

"There is nothing either good or bad, but thinking makes it so."
—WILLIAM SHAKESPEARE

TRUE STORY: Sam Walton: "How Can We Improve?"

One of the best examples of a businessperson who embodied continual improvement is Sam Walton, founder of Wal-Mart.

Years ago, the *Wall Street Journal* printed an excellent article about how the sales of Wal-Mart, a small-town Arkansas company, has beaten Kmart, a national powerhouse, year after year in an undeclared retailing war.

In an extremely well-researched article, the authors turned over many rocks looking for the key reason for Wal-Mart's success. Among some of the reasons they identified were customer focus—perhaps better described as an "obsession," but a healthy and profitable obsession—and superior systems for processing business effectively.

However, at the end of the article, the two writers came up with what they believed to be the most important element in Wal-Mart's success:

"In the end attitude may have made a bigger difference than strategy. In Bentonville, Mr. Walton and Mr. Glass asked subordinates what was not working and chided them for failing to deliver any bad news." (March 24, 1995)

Improve your performance first; profits will follow.

Recognize what's important here: A CEO is walking into his store and asking people what's not working! He's not trying to deny anything or sweep problems under the rug. He is reaching out to his people and asking how their operations could be improved. When his associates did not make suggestions, Walton *chided* them for failing to deliver any bad news. Obviously, getting the real story was more important to him than hearing that everything was just fine.

According to the *Wall Street Journal* article, Walton's counterpart at Kmart did the exact opposite. Not only did he not actively seek out the bad news from his staff, he turned a deaf ear even when his staff came to him with obvious opportunities to improve. He seemed to prefer to attend photo opportunities instead of determining how his company could improve. The result was that, two weeks before Christmas, his distribution centers were filled with products while his stores were empty. Try explaining that to your clients, associates and shareholders.

This article shows just how important attitude is. You'd be hard pressed to find a better example than Sam Walton of a businessperson with an excellent attitude. Wal-Mart's success speaks for itself. Walton started with one store in 1945 and parlayed it into an international retailing giant that continues to thrive years after his death.

Finally, listen carefully to what Walton did not say: "Let's beat Kmart sales; let's squeeze more money from the customers," or "Let's make more money for our stockholders." He said none of that. Instead he focused on continual improvement: "Where can we improve? What can we do better?" This focus on continual improvement brought financial returns that wowed everyone, including Walton.

QUESTIONS FOR YOU

- *How much more successful and profitable will you be when you follow Walton's example by constantly asking, "How can we improve?"*
- *How specifically can you improve?*
- *On a scale of 1 to 10, how open are you to continual improvement?*
- *Are you constantly soliciting feedback from your associates and clients?*

Continual Improvement: Daily

The greatest motivation must come from within you. You can hear motivational speakers day in and day out and read all the books under the sun (as I have). But ultimately, continual improvement must begin with you. You must embrace and live an attitude of continual improvement. Begin today to live by a simple philosophy: "I'm good but I want to be better."

Just preaching an attitude of continual improvement is not enough. If you are a leader in a company, you yourself must live a philosophy of continual improvement every day. Others will be motivated by your actions, not empty words.

I regularly visit a variety of business offices and see all sorts of motivational statements on the walls. Some companies think all they need to do is put a half-dozen posters on the wall and they will achieve what the posters suggest. I have found that it's often the companies with those posters on the wall that are least likely to practice the strategies.

You must institute concrete actions on a daily basis to prove to yourself, your co-workers and your clients that you are committed to continual improvement. Your actions must match your desire to improve.

You improve a behavior only when you measure it.

Measure, Measure, Measure to Improve, Improve, Improve!

Once you have refocused your attitude, the final step toward achieving daily continual improvement is measuring and improving your performance. Think about it. When you want to lose weight, you weigh yourself and measure your food intake. When you want to improve your golf game, you honestly track your strokes, how many times you hit the ball. Why not apply this same strategy to your business endeavors? How do you know if you are improving in business unless you are measuring your performance? When you want to improve any behavior, begin measuring it.

Day in and day out, I see all types of businesses missing valuable opportunities to improve by not properly measuring and sharing various performances. If American businesses measured their performance as American sports teams do, fewer would go into bankruptcy.

How Measuring Improves Performance

GoalStar's workshops improved dramatically

when I asked on my feedback forms, "On a scale of 1 to 10, with 1 being the worst and 10 being the best, where do you rank this workshop?"

The follow-up question was equally important: "If this workshop is not a 10, what can be done to make it a 10?"

By measuring performance and soliciting feedback, I accomplished the following:

I put myself on notice that my performance was being measured. Do not underestimate the importance of putting yourself on notice. I focused even more on the quality of workshops knowing that I was asking participants to assess my performance.

I gained many valuable strategies for improvement. People love to give advice, so why not take advantage of it? I just kept rolling all the great ideas I picked up into the workshops—"include this," "restructure this," "tell us more about that," "do a section on this." Some of the most popular workshop topics have come from these workshop feedback forms.

In short, when I started measuring workshops, the quality dramatically improved.

If you have any area in your business that you want to improve, begin to measure it. Don't be concerned about whether your measurements are exact. Just begin to measure; you will fine-tune your system as you go along.

QUESTION FOR YOU

- *How much more successful and profitable will you be when you measure and analyze your performance?*

Competing Against Yourself

Most owners and managers forget that their greatest challenge in business is not the competition but rather *complacency* and *mediocrity*. They become so consumed with their competitors and other external factors that they neglect to look inside themselves and their businesses. *The greatest opportunity for growth is inward.*

To improve, compete against your own previous performance.

The Japanese achieved great success when, instead of competing against Detroit, they competed against themselves. I was much more effective and found greater satisfaction in my work when I competed against my own performance rather than against others in my office or against rival companies. When I stopped focusing on others and just concerned myself with my own performance, I made great strides.

Perhaps Wal-Mart gives us the best example of a company that has effectively competed against itself. When Sam Walton ran the company, he asked that every store post in the back what that store's previous sales had been on the same day one year before. He did not post Kmart's sales or those of other Wal-Mart stores; he encouraged stores to compete against their own previous performances.

Did it work? Wal-Mart's blistering record of sales growth attest to the fact that it did.

For many businesspeople, competing against themselves is a novel concept. Everyone is concerned about competing against others. But when you want to be really successful, compete against yourself. Be focused on constant, never-ending improvement.

If you are a manager, inspire your team to compete against last month's performance numbers. If you are in sales, post last month's or last year's sales and use them as an incentive. Even if you are not in sales, you can still measure performance. Companies can and should compete against themselves in customer service and accounting. If you're in accounting, track how many transactions you completed the previous month or that month the year before. If you are in customer service, track daily and weekly customer calls or shipments, and compare these figures with the previous month's and previous year's.

Track how many clients call your office daily and why they call.

TRUE STORY: How Measuring Performance Can Alter Perceptions

I recently completed a consulting project with a customer-service call center that fielded anywhere from 1,200 to 1,800 calls daily, with only eight to ten people answering the telephones! Obviously, this was quite a challenge. In an effort to stem the number of incoming calls and better serve clients, I suggested tracking exactly why clients were calling.

The pie chart shown on page 42 represents one typical day of this client's calls. To say that the customer service representatives were surprised that almost half the calls—45 percent—were customers wanting to *start* service would be an understatement. They thought the majority of customers were calling to complain.

By tracking and sharing data like that in the pie chart with the customer service reps weekly, we significantly altered their perception of their work. Rather than feeling that all customer calls were complaints, customer service reps began to see the positive results of what they were doing.

"CALL TABULATION" CHANGED PERCEPTIONS

THIS PIE CHART shows the results of one day's tabulation of customer phone calls by a waste-management company. It analyzed its calls daily and communicated the results in an easily understood format. The company thereby hoped to reveal why customers were calling, and to improve customer service representatives' morale and the quality of their service. The big surprise for everyone? The majority of callers wanted to *start* service, not complain about it.

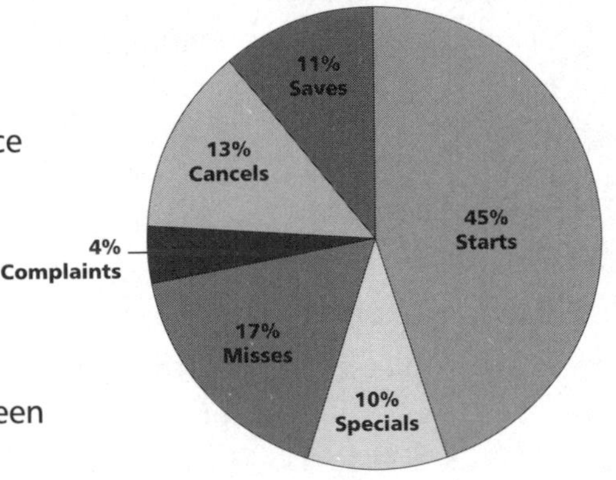

KEY TO THE CHART

Starts: Request to start service

Specials: Customers who wanted to schedule special pick-ups

Misses: Customers who called to say that they had been missed on the daily routes

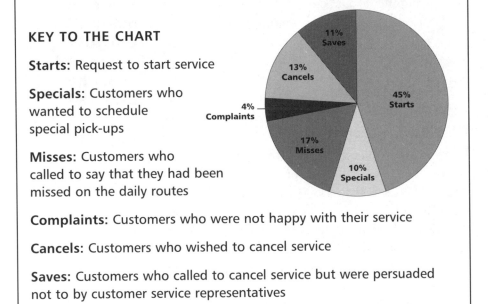

Complaints: Customers who were not happy with their service

Cancels: Customers who wished to cancel service

Saves: Customers who called to cancel service but were persuaded not to by customer service representatives

The majority of clients were not complaining; they were signing up for new business.

Analyzing why clients were calling was the first step toward improving performance. Next, we developed an ongoing customer service training program to continually sharpen the representatives' skills. What was once a reactive group became a proactive and profitable team. The customer service reps' morale and their ability to properly serve clients improved significantly when they saw this analysis of their daily calls.

QUESTIONS FOR YOU

- *What performance in your organization can you significantly improve by tracking and sharing data?*
- *Whose morale in your organization can you improve by sharing data?*
- *How much more successful and profitable will your organization be because of sharing this valuable information?*

Give clients project or transaction status before they request it.

Putting Together the Three Continual Improvement Strategies

If you are skeptical about whether these three continual improvement strategies work (practicing LB/NT, continually improving your attitude and measuring your performance) let me share an example of how I used all three to overcome my fear of public speaking.

Oddly enough for someone who makes his living speaking to groups, I used to be terrified of public speaking. Actually, "terrified" is an understatement. In school, I avoided all classes that required an oral report. In business, I would duck out of large meetings if I had to introduce myself. If I ever ended up speaking publicly because I could not avoid it (and, boy, did I try), I would get all worked up. I couldn't breathe, my palms would sweat, and my stomach would churn. Public speaking paralyzed me. Whenever I spoke, I wanted to be off stage as quickly as possible.

I had such a fear of public speaking that I knew I had to overcome it. My fear was causing me to miss opportunities that could bring me greater opportunity and fulfillment. I had to change my attitude about public speaking—to face it and overcome my fear.

I started small, with a one-on-one speech class, working on reading aloud to another person. Reading aloud, in front of others, had been a phobia of mine for as long as I could remember. After a month, my fears began to subside. I began to feel more comfortable reading aloud to my public-speaking coach.

To improve public speaking, join Toastmasters (www.toastmasters.org).

Then the coach recommended that I take a class on speaking phobias, designed for people just like me who became paralyzed at the thought of public speaking. It turned out to be one of the best classes I have taken.

From the class I learned many practical strategies for public speaking—such as arriving ahead of time to familiarize myself with the room and become comfortable in it—and the importance of practicing, practicing and practicing my talk. Perhaps the most valuable thing I learned was that many other people had a similar fear of public speaking. I was not alone. Somehow knowing this made it easier to work on improving my public-speaking skills.

Taking this public-speaking class enabled me to become much more comfortable in front of a group of people—OK, 12 people, but that was 11 more than I had been comfortable in front of before. I was making progress.

The class went well, and one of the teachers made another recommendation to me—Toastmasters, an international organization dedicated to helping people improve their public-speaking skills. Not only is this organization an excellent forum for practicing and honing your speaking skills, but it also gives you the most sympathetic audience of speaking coaches you'll ever find. You will be hard pressed to find another audience that wants to see you succeed more and is also capable of sharing many practical tools to improve your public-speaking skills. In short, Toastmasters is a great environment in which to overcome a fear of public speaking and improve your skills. (You can reach the group on the Internet at www.toastmasters.org.)

Every time you don't analyze your performance, you miss a valuable opportunity to improve.

Toastmasters did wonders for my confidence. I found myself in front of 15 to 20 people and no longer consumed by fear. Now, I was more concerned about clearly and completely articulating my points, a rewarding shift of perspective.

By the time I started speaking for a living, I had gained much but still had a lot to learn. Here I used the two other strategies for continual improvement.

Liked Best, Next Time

After every talk I gave, I analyzed my performance by doing a "Liked Best, Next Time" exercise. I asked myself what I liked best about my presentation. I also asked how, specifically, I could improve next time. Later, I found greater success by rating my presentation on a scale of 1 to 10.

Measuring Performance

I realized that when I spoke to a group, I was in front of an audience of speaking coaches. Everyone loves to give his or her opinion, so I decided not to miss another valuable opportunity for improvement.

Whether I spoke to five people or 500, if I could pick up at least one suggestion for improve-

GOALSTAR CONTINUAL IMPROVEMENT

DATE ____________________

COMPANY X—"Keeping Clients for Life"

NAME (optional) ____________________

What did you learn from today's workshop that you can apply immediately?

1. ____________________
2. ____________________
3. ____________________
4. ____________________
5. ____________________
6. ____________________

Did this workshop meet, not meet, or exceed your expectations? Why or why not? ____________________

____

On a scale from 1 to 10, with 10 being best, this workshop was a ____________.

If not a 10, how can this workshop be improved or made more enjoyable? ____________________

____

What sections were the best? ____________________

____

What sections need improvement? ____________________

____

What other issues or topics can we cover to help you be more successful? ____________________

____

ment, I was ahead of the game. Here also was another opportunity to use one of the continual-improvement strategies I've described in this chapter—that of measuring performance.

Every time I spoke, no matter how big or small the audience, I had available a GoalStar Continual Improvement form, so that the audience could critique my performance. I have included a copy on the preceding page.

Asking targeted questions produces more accurate data.

Using the form, I asked specifically the following question: How can this workshop be improved or made more enjoyable?

I read all the responses carefully and began a folder for all the feedback forms from all of my speaking engagements. Sometimes before a big presentation, I still read through the folder for improvement reminders.

As I read more and more feedback forms, I realized I needed to ask more targeted questions to get even more accurate data. For example, I added questions like:

- **What sections were the best?**
- **What sections need improvement?**
- **Did the workshop meet, not meet, or exceed your expectations?**
- **On a scale of 1 to 10, with 10 being best, where does this workshop fall?**

The bottom line is that not only has my public speaking improved quickly, but also my business has grown.

Besides implementing the three continual-improvement strategies, I learned two more lessons from overcoming my fear of public speaking. First, if you're afraid of public speaking, do something about it today. Do what I did and start small. Join Toastmasters to overcome your fear.

Second, life is about expressing yourself clearly and persuading others. Why not avail yourself of all the tools you can so you can be your most persuasive? If you can effectively persuade a large group of people, how much more effective and persuasive will you be with a smaller group?

Lifetime Tool 1 is simple. Before a client, boss or co-worker tells you how to improve, ask yourself how you can improve. Wherever you work in an organization, always be open to learning and growing. You can always improve. I am a much improved speaker now because I was willing to learn and I reached out and asked for help.

Always strive to be honest and give your best efforts.

When you want to earn lifetime clients, begin by first asking yourself how you can improve.

THINGS TO DO "MONDAY MORNING"

- **Be a lifetime student.** Always be open to learning and growing.
- **After every client encounter,** ask yourself what you did well and how you can improve.
- **Compete against yourself** and your own previous performances.
- **Measure and analyze** your performance.

Properly Preparing Yourself to Win the Lifetime Relationship

LIFETIME TOOL

2

CUSTOMER ONCE, CLIENT FOREVER

In this chapter, I'll share:

- **The importance of understanding your market and your place in that market**
- **The importance of completely understanding your products and services**
- **The importance of knowing your competition**
- **The four client needs**

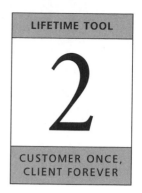

In our instant gratification society, we are trained to want and expect everything immediately. Some people may think that lifetime clients come instantly, too. They don't. Perhaps you have heard that wonderful adage, "It takes years to win a client, seconds to lose one." It can take literally years to win a lifetime relationship.

Just as you build a building by laying the proper foundation, floor by floor, you must lay a similar foundation if you are going to build lifetime client relationships. Before you can effectively serve your clients, you need to completely understand the market in which you do business, the products and services you offer, and the strengths and weaknesses of your competition. To best achieve a lifetime relationship with your clients, you want to be considered their trusted adviser. Before they'll trust your advice, you must become an expert in your field. If you demonstrate your expertise, why would clients want to talk with anyone else? You have provided them with a wealth of information.

By understanding your market and your clients' needs, you can not only better promote your own products and services, but also give advice to your clients that goes beyond what your company normally offers. You can help your clients be more successful and profitable, which in turn will increase your business as your partnership strengthens.

We'll address these strategies more specifically in Lifetime Tool 4, Superserving Your Client.

Understand Your Market

Become the expert in your field.

To fully understand a client's needs, you must completely understand the market in which you compete and your place in that market. What drives your market? What makes your market special or unique? What makes your firm special? Why would a client want to do business with you? What unique services do you offer?

What I mean by market is the nature of your business. Is it seasonal? Is it sensitive to changes in the economy? Or is your business like the funeral industry, where demand tends to be steady no matter what the health of the rest of the economy?

I find most businesspeople do only half the work here. They develop a comfort level with industry information, then try to sell clients. I am suggesting that you go two, three and four steps further. Do the homework. The financial return will repay your effort over and over again. And as I've mentioned before, because of your superior knowledge, clients will seek you out.

Use three strategies to help you understand your market better:

1. Always ask all your clients, "How's business?" Listen to what they tell you. Look for commonalities and trends. You will learn a great deal if you listen to your clients and their views on the market. To gain more information, when appropriate without violating confidentiality, share with clients what other clients are doing and have done.

2. Follow up on all projects you've bid or worked on, especially the ones you think you might have lost. You want to know to whom the project ultimately went and how your competitor performed. You especially want to know—and this is where most businesspeople drop the ball—whether clients were happy with the service, and whether their expectations were met or exceeded.

Know your business well enough to offer clients options.

3. Continuously educate yourself on your industry. Read all you can on your market in newspapers and trade publications. Attend networking events, lectures and seminars. Surf the Web. The point is to keep current with the trends in your industry. And read between the lines: Develop a discerning eye to what are truly trends and what are misfires. This takes time and experience.

To become a trusted adviser, you must do the research. In short, consider yourself a reporter who is preparing an article on your industry to be printed on the front page of a national newspaper.

QUESTIONS FOR YOU

- *How well do you know your industry?*
- *If a reporter called you to interview you about your industry, would you be able to speak intelligently, articulately and comfortably?*

Understand All Your Products and Services

In addition to knowing your market, you must know your products and services inside and out. No matter how long you have been with an organization, you should continually improve your product and service knowledge.

I recently met with representatives of a major consulting firm and learned that their firm had 43 lines of business. I bet that if you had interviewed a smattering of the firm's people, only a few would have been able to intelligently and accurately describe all 43 lines of business.

Continually sharpen your product and service knowledge.

In today's rapidly changing business environment, you must keep up with all the services your firm offers clients. If you are a manager or an owner, you need to continually educate your associates on all your services. If you are an associate, you need to continually sharpen your product and service knowledge.

If you have a choice between attending a fluffy sales seminar or a real training opportunity on your products or services, attend the product training and use this knowledge to provide greater value to your clients.

The bottom line is that the better you know your products and services and the more you become an expert in your field, the more people will seek you out. You will not have to chase clients for business; they will be calling you because of your expertise.

As I've said before, when clients bother to track you down, rarely is price an issue. They're coming to you because they want your knowledge and experience.

QUESTIONS FOR YOU

- *How well do you know all your products and services?*
- *How are you continually sharpening your product and service knowledge?*

Understand Your Competition

In addition to knowing their markets, the most successful businesspeople understand their competition. Not only do they know who they are, they specifically know how the competition stacks up against their own business in terms of price, service, expertise, and delivery. Through experience, they also know competitors' shortcomings. Some businesspeople, for whatever reasons, avoid their competitors—or flat out dismiss them: "Oh, they don't know what they're doing."

Learn as much as you can about your competition.

I suggest you go the other way. Just as I suggested in the first chapter that you embrace your perceived weaknesses, I now suggest that you embrace your competitors. Get to know them. Who are they? How long have they been in business? What do their clients say about them? What are their strengths? Where do they fall short? Finding the answers will only make you stronger and allow you to serve your clients better.

Learning about your competitors doesn't give you license to demean them. Successful businesspeople never demean the competition. The best businesspeople I have seen always acknowledge the competition's strengths and are careful about pointing out a shortcoming. You will win a lifetime relationship with a client not by tearing down and criticizing the competition but by providing outstanding and continuing value to your clients.

You can learn about competitors and possibly earn business by staying in touch with businesses that have not accepted your previous proposals and went elsewhere for help.

Attend seminars given by competitors to see the information they give out and mail out. Not only will you learn about the competition by reviewing this information, but you might also discover effective and creative strategies to reach your clients.

Consider establishing a dialogue with competitors. Sharing information may help them but, if you're shrewd, you will also learn better ways to reach clients. When you accomplish this, everyone wins—clients, competitors and you.

Walk forever in your clients' shoes.

The better you know your competitors and the more current the information you have on them, the more success you will have. You don't win lifetime relationships just by blindsiding the competition; you win by providing clients superior products and service.

For instance, a client of mine once attended a competing firm's seminar with me and was surprised at how inferior the material was. My client gives a detailed and precise two-hour lecture on financial planning with a question-and-answer period at the end. His competitor gave a 45-minute meandering talk complete with color slide show that glossed over all the main points but was filled with many veiled sales pitches. My client leaned over to me during the presentation and said, "So this is the competition?"

By taking time to research the competition, my client recognized the added value he was bringing to his potential clients. The next time he was in front of his clients, he had a renewed faith and confidence. He knew he was giving clients real value.

As I followed up on projects that I had lost, I developed a greater awareness of the strengths and shortcomings of my competition. I started to excel in business because I developed a greater awareness about which competitors could properly serve clients and which ones could not. In short, I developed a much greater understanding of the entire marketplace. This newfound understanding allowed me to better serve clients and increase profitability.

QUESTIONS FOR YOU

- *Are you learning about your competition?*
- *How well do you understand your competition?*

Always seek to educate clients, not to sell them.

TRUE STORY: How Understanding My Competition Helped Me to Win a Large Contract

Ten years ago, I was working for a company that bid a large contract to an out-of-town developer building a local apartment complex. We had submitted a $150,000 bid, which the general contractor had accepted.

This had been a particularly involved sale. We were fortunate to be called in by the general contractor 18 months before the actual bid to help write the specifications for the job. Having taken the time to help write the specifications, we definitely wanted that sale. After much hard work and negotiation with the general contractor, we won the contract, or so I thought.

A couple of months after our bid was accepted, we learned that the owner had pulled our portion out of the general contractor's bid and would put that portion out for bid himself. Nothing like having a $150,000 contract taken out from under you!

We aggressively pursued the developer and found ourselves in a hotly contested race. What was once a solid $150,000 contract had become a slugfest with an out-of-town competitor. Time was of the essence—the client wanted the project completed by the first of the year, and it was already October. I had never heard of this competitor. I knew it had not completed a major project in our area. In addition, its bid was $40,000 less than mine on the project, 2,500 miles from its office. In short, I seriously doubted whether it could successfully complete the project.

Never demean your competition.

We went back and forth on the price. The client wanted to be at $110,000, which was too low for us. We wondered how an out-of-town firm could come to our area and bid a very labor-intensive project so low.

Experience had taught me not to burn any bridges, so I let the project go without making any disparaging comments, such as "it can't be done." We didn't get nasty or upset or whine to the client about all the specification work we had done. We were disappointed, but we didn't express this to the client.

The day before Thanksgiving, I was at home with the flu when the developer called to say he was caught between a rock and a hard place. Our competitor could not do the job for the price, and the developer wanted us out on the site as soon as possible to measure and order the material. He needed to have our contract completed by Christmas, less than one month away, an almost impossible request.

Through a total team effort by our firm, our suppliers and our trucking companies, we did it. Our client was extremely happy.

I learned a great deal from this experience. It was an opportunity to make a profit on what turned out to be a $120,000 contract. While the profit was not as much as we had hoped for, it was still a profit.

More important, we developed a lifetime client. While we did not make all the profit we wanted to initially, we made it all up, and then some, in the repeat business we subsequently did for the client.

That experience confirmed for me the importance of not bad-mouthing the competition or saying the company couldn't succeed. It also reminded me of the importance of keeping the door wide open for clients to return without any loss of face.

Make sure you and your clients clearly understand their needs.

Lastly, it reinforced my commitment to serving my clients. I left the project with greater confidence in our firm's ability to serve a client. In all future projects, I was more confident than ever before that we could meet and exceed client expectations even under the most demanding circumstances.

Understand the Four Client Needs

Now that you have done the legwork by completely understanding your marketplace, your products and services, and the competition, let's turn our focus to your clients. Specifically, your clients have four needs. The better you understand these four needs, the better you can serve them.

As we discussed, your goal in business is to become a trusted adviser. Clients should implicitly trust your judgment. You want your clients to call only you. You should be their ultimate resource. They may talk to others, but they want to do business with you. How do you achieve this enviable position? By recognizing your clients' four needs:

1. Your product or service
2. A fair price
3. Outstanding service
4. A lifetime relationship

When you recognize and properly respond to these four needs, you are well on your way to developing a lifetime client relationship.

Anticipate your clients' needs. Call clients before they have to track you down.

1. Your Product or Service

What prompted the person to call you? Or, as a client of mine says, "Where's the pain?" If you sell cars, your client wants to buy a car. If you are a real estate agent, your client wants to buy or sell a home, or both. If you are in hotel reservations, your client wants a room. If you are a financial adviser, your client wants to make money and plan for the future. Those are the clients' needs at their simplest.

I find that most businesses do only an adequate job of understanding the complete client need. What exact type of car is he looking for? What type of retirement or insurance plan is she seeking? What type of home does he want? The more completely we understand clients' need—or pain, as my client above would refer to it—the better we can serve them. To understand client needs, you need to listen carefully and ask good questions.

The greatest opportunity your company has today is to become closer to your clients, that is, to completely understand all the challenges your clients face. The more you understand client needs, the better you can serve these needs. The better you serve client needs, the more clients will come to you. Your business will grow exponentially. Let's share an example of how IBM is getting closer to its clients.

TRUE STORY: IBM and Its Clients' Needs

In the summer of 1998 the *New York Times* business section ran an interesting article about the research side of IBM. In the past, IBM research has not connected closely with clients' needs. In fact, the article quoted an internal analysis showing that at the start of the 1990s only 2 percent to 5 percent of the research division work went toward specific products and services for IBM customers.

Completely understand your clients' needs, and then exceed them.

The article described how IBM has made headway closing this gap by developing products and services that better meet client needs. There is still great opportunity for IBM to become even closer to clients' needs. For example, during a recent brainstorming session, a group of IBM executives, researchers and summer interns were encouraged to think like their clients. They were asked to come with products and services to sell to companies like Coca-Cola, Levi Strauss, Citibank and Disney.

Look carefully at what IBM did. They asked their people to think like their clients, a good start.

What keeps IBM from going one critical step further and asking their clients directly: "What are your greatest technological challenges? How can we help you be more successful and profitable?"

While IBM should be congratulated for its efforts, how much more effective and profitable will IBM be when it partners with its clients and asks them what specific technology challenges they face and how IBM can assist them? Why think up client challenges when you can ask clients directly what challenges they face? When you are asking clients questions like these, you are making giant strides toward building a lifetime partnership.

What would happen if next year IBM approached these companies before its brainstorming sessions and said it wanted to partner with them and help them solve their most pressing business and information-technology questions? What type of response would IBM get from its clients? How much more effective would its brainstorming sessions be?

Ask clients what their most pressing concerns are, and then ask how you can best assist them.

The moral of this story is that IBM can do a better job understanding client needs.

No matter where you work in a company, you can always improve your understanding of clients' needs. The chapters on listening (Lifetime Tool 6) and on asking the right questions (Lifetime Tool 7) are designed to give you concrete approaches to better understanding client needs.

If some businesspeople find this first level of client needs challenging, the vast majority miss the next three.

QUESTIONS FOR YOU

- *How well do you really understand your clients' needs?*
- *If you are a president or manager, how do you properly measure whether your people are truly and completely understanding your clients' needs?*

2. Fair Price

Whether in sales, customer service, technical assistance or management, companies have a challenging time walking in their clients' shoes. They fail to recognize that clients want a fair price and want to be treated well. Clients don't want to be taken advantage of or *feel* as if they are being taken advantage of. Clients want to pay the best possible price and still receive outstanding service. There is no worse feeling than knowing that you overpaid for a product or service. Having clients feel that they overpaid for a service is one sure-fire way *not* to build a lifetime relationship. We've talked about being the trusted adviser. Part of a trusted adviser's role is to provide clients with pricing information, that is, to advise clients of the fees and capital investments associated with certain products and services.

Develop lifetime clients by pricing your products and services fairly.

Pricing is a very sensitive issue. We'll offer specific questions in Lifetime Tool 8 that will help you advise a client in the pricing area. In short, to build lifetime clients, price your products and services fairly.

3. Outstanding Service

You'll never hear a client say, "You know, I really drove you hard on the price, so it's all right to give me mediocre service." No matter what the fee, clients always want outstanding service. Surprised?

In fact, I find that the harder clients push for a good price, the more service they expect. If you ask your clients whether they want good service or a low price, they will always answer, "Both." That's a given. Don't fight it. If you give them both consistently, you'll have your clients for a lifetime.

Treating clients fairly and delivering outstanding service makes clients want to return with repeat business or refer others to you.

Too often I see clients "limping" out of offices while the businesspeople "high-five" each other in the background. Yes, those businesspeople have won the battle because they made a sale. However, they lost the war because they will not have the lifetime relationship.

In short, always deliver outstanding service. Outstanding service is what brings clients back. I think delivering outstanding service is so important that I've dedicated an entire chapter to it—Lifetime Tool Number 8, Systemizing Your Business.

QUESTION FOR YOU

Always provide outstanding service.

- *If you are president or manager, how do you measure whether clients are receiving excellent service?*

4. A Lifetime Relationship

Whether you realize it or not, your clients want someone whose judgment they implicitly trust, someone who they feel is on their side, someone to whom they can refer others. Remember, people love to refer friends to their "special person."

Do you think that every time clients need a product or service, they want to go out on the street and try to find someone new to trust? Do you think every time they buy a home, they want to hunt around for a reliable real estate agent? Do you think they want to risk one of the biggest investments they have with an unproven entity? The same is true of financial planners and brokers.

This may be a surprise to you, but guess what your clients want? They want a lifetime relationship. Why wouldn't they? Clients want someone they can trust completely and call anytime. Clients want a trusted adviser they can send others to. They want someone they can always depend on.

Let me share how I was reminded of this lesson in the middle of a heat wave.

In the middle of June, in Washington, D.C., with temperatures in the high 90s, the air conditioning goes out at my home. My first thought is that the whole system needs to be replaced. Not only will it be expensive, I will be without air conditioning during the hottest days of the summer. It's actually hotter inside than it is outside. So my mind is occupied with two thoughts: How many thousands of dollars will a new system cost? And how will I stay cool in all this heat?

Be proactive, not reactive.

I don't know whom to call. My system was serviced more than seven years ago, and I cannot locate the firm that performed the service. So I call around for quality referrals. Before I hire anyone, I want to make sure he does outstanding work.

The two best referrals are booked solid. I finally get someone who can come out the next morning. The technician, whom I'll call Bob, is very knowledgeable. It turns out the system is frozen and needs to thaw. So we need to wait another day to find out what is wrong. Of course, that means another day of temperatures in the 90s.

After four days of no air conditioning and record heat, Bob takes me down to the basement and shows me that my filters are pitch black. The filters have not been cleaned in seven years, and have shut down the entire system.

Bob replaces the filters and restarts the system. What I thought might be a thousand-dollar expense is handled for less than $150.

I relate the story above to make the simple point that I wish the firm that had cleaned the filters seven years ago had adopted me as a lifetime client. Then, the firm could have called or sent a card that said it was time to check my filters. It could have called to schedule a visit. It may have even gone so far as to offer me a maintenance contract. If the firm had done that, I would not have had a shutdown during the hottest days of summer. In addition to my referring the firm to others, it most likely would have been my first choice to replace my existing system when the time comes.

Bottom line, to build a lifetime client relationship, you must always be aware that your clients have four needs:

1. **Your product or service**
2. **A fair price**
3. **Outstanding service**
4. **A lifetime relationship**

Recognize that your clients need your expertise and service.

QUESTIONS FOR YOU

- *Do you completely understand clients' needs?*
- *Are you pricing your products and services properly?*
- *Are you delivering outstanding service?*

Becoming the Trusted Adviser

You can summarize this chapter into one simple strategy: Position yourself as a trusted adviser to your clients. With all the information you learn about the market, your services and your clients' complete needs, you, much like a doctor, are in a unique position to advise your clients.

This strategy of being the trusted adviser is absolutely critical to your success in achieving lifetime clients. Business today is not about selling clients, it's about advising clients. Your role is not to sell but to educate clients on all the options available to them. Being the trusted adviser is not about what's in it for you, it's about providing long-term value to your clients.

When I "sold" to my clients, I had one level of

success. When I became the trusted adviser, I had three times the success. And as I mentioned, clients chased me! I didn't have to market my services. I just had to continually improve my service. In the next chapter, I'll discuss how you complete this trusted adviser positioning to be of maximum value to your clients.

Be in business for your clients.

THINGS TO DO "MONDAY MORNING"

- **Constantly educate yourself on your market.** Scour trade journals, Web sites and other valuable sources of information. Stay current!
- **Continually sharpen your product and service knowledge.** Be well versed in all your products and service lines.
- **Know your competitors.** Go to their Web sites and any public seminars they offer to check out their products and marketing vehicles. Ask your clients about experiences they've had with the competition.
- **Stay in touch with all clients to whom you've given proposals,** whether they've accepted them or not.

Chasing the Client, Not the Dollar

LIFETIME TOOL

3

CUSTOMER ONCE, CLIENT FOREVER

In this chapter, I'll share:

- **The primary purpose of being in business**
- **Why successful companies measure their success by what's important to their clients**
- **A broader definition of business success**

This chapter offers the simplest principles in this book: Be in business for your clients and exceed their expectations. While these principles are simple, they may be the most challenging to apply consistently, because most businesses are consumed with making a profit. When you completely embrace and implement this client-first, profit-second philosophy, you will achieve greater success and fulfillment as well as substantially increase your profits.

Why are you in business? Is your primary purpose to make money or to serve your client? If you are in business strictly to make money, you will achieve one level of success. If you are in business to exceed clients' expectations, you will achieve a higher level of success, one that is much more rewarding.

This doesn't mean you will forgo making a profit. As I've said before, you can't stay in business if you don't make a profit. I believe in profit so much that I devoted an entire chapter to how to best serve clients and maximize profits (Lifetime Tool 8, Systemizing Your Business). However, by focusing first on exceeding client expectations and then on making profits, you will generate greater sales and higher profits.

Happy clients are loyal clients. They'll keep coming back to you and recommend you to all their associates, if you demonstrate to them consistently that your primary concern is keeping them happy.

No matter where you work in a company, you always have the opportunity to serve clients. You constantly need to ask yourself: Am I serving my clients' needs or my needs? To build lifetime relationships, always put client needs ahead of your needs. When you put client needs first, you will achieve long-term business success.

Aim at the right target: clients first, profits second.

Perhaps this client-first philosophy is best illustrated by an example, using two catalog companies.

TRUE STORY: Two Catalog Companies—A & B

You call Catalog Company A to order one of its products. The customer service representative answers the telephone somewhat abruptly and abrasively, and asks you the following questions:

1. **"What is your billing address?"**
2. **"What credit card will you be using?"**
3. **"What is your credit card number and expiration date?"**
4. **"What is your ship-to address?"**
5. **"What is the key number and catalog number on the back of the catalog?**

In five minutes of your telephone time, the customer service representative has collected five pieces of information about billing, but she has not asked you why you called nor asked you for your order. The company, judging by its representative, seems concerned only about getting paid, not about meeting your needs. After you have given her all this information, she'd better have what you want in stock!

You call a second catalog company. The client service representative at Company B answers the telephone in a polite and friendly manner, identifying herself. As she opens her computer order screen, she asks how the weather is in your part of the country. She tells you how pretty it is on the West Coast, where she is. Continuing in that same friendly yet professional tone, she asks the following questions:

Consistently exceed client expectations, and profits will follow.

1. **"What can I get for you today, Mr. Buckingham?"** (Using the client's name is a nice touch.)
2. **"How many of these would you like?"** (This is a great question. If you want to increase business immediately, start asking this question.)
3. **"May I do anything else for you today?"** (Another great question.)

Only now does she get the billing information she needs to complete the sale:

4. **"What credit card will you be using today?"**
5. **"What is your credit card number and expiration date?"**
6. **"Are your billing and ship-to addresses the same?"**
7. **"If these items ship the first of the week, will that be satisfactory?"** (Another nice touch.)

Two similar transactions. Two completely different impressions made on the client. The first company came across concerned first with profit, not with serving client needs. It wanted billing and payment information before the actual order information. The second company wanted the order first, then the billing information, which implied it was more interested in the client's concerns (placing the order) than the company's concerns (receiving payment).

QUESTIONS FOR YOU

- *Which catalog company would you be more likely to order from again?*
- *Which firm has a greater chance of developing a lifetime relationship with its clients?*
- *Are you chasing the dollar or the client?*

Profit is the by-product of outstanding work.

TRUE STORY: I Was Company A

I take you through this example because when I first started in business, I was Company A in the scenario above. I put my needs in front of my clients'. I was concerned only about the single transaction and the profit from that single transaction. All my initial sales were transactional instead of relational. Money, not the relationship, was the bottom line.

I didn't have the wisdom or experience to see the importance of a lifetime client relationship or the value and ease of repeat and referral business. All I cared about was that first sale. I tried to wring as much as I could from the transaction and move on. Needless to say, my sales and my job satisfaction were limited.

As I wised up, I started to see and understand clients' needs. Every client I came in contact with had a need. The better I understood and served these needs, the more fulfillment I received from my work and the more future business I received.

This shift from putting my own concerns first to putting my clients' concerns first made all the difference in the world. I started to listen more closely to clients (Lifetime Tool 6) to make sure I completely understood what they were looking for and to make sure that my products and services actually fit their needs. I also started asking better questions (Lifetime Tool 7) to understand clients' needs so I could best serve them.

I see the concern—or perhaps a better word is obsession—for profit over service plaguing most American businesses. Most companies seem to be obsessed with short-term profit. They care only about how much they can wring from a client, not about how they can properly serve that client's needs and develop a lifetime relationship. Businesses attempt to make their money on the turnover of clients—bring in a new one, bleed him for money, let him go, and bring in the next one.

Every single action you take must be in your clients' best interests.

Most businesses measure their "success" in terms of their own sales and profitability, not in terms of client satisfaction or lifetime relationships. This is a very short-sighted and skewed view. Unfortunately, few businesses measure their success by overall client satisfaction, percentage of repeat and referral business, or other indicators that are important to clients. I'll offer a broader definition of success in a couple of pages. Let's talk now about the profit-first philosophy.

QUESTION FOR YOU

- *How much more profitable will you be when you broaden your definition of success?*

What's Wrong With the Profit-First Philosophy?

Companies that put profit first fail to realize that if they shift their primary focus from profit to serving and exceeding clients' needs, they will not only gain short-term profit but also set themselves up for long-term success.

While profit is a healthy goal of any businessperson, it shouldn't be the primary goal. That's putting the cart before the horse. If you focus your efforts first on exceeding your clients' needs, profitability will follow. And when you exceed clients' needs, you'll be making money hand over fist. As I've suggested, clients will beat down your door to do business with you.

Make your business relational, not transactional.

My sales doubled and tripled when, instead of obsessing about what I gained from clients, I focused on exceeding their needs. When I put client needs ahead of mine, I couldn't control all the new clients pursuing me.

In addition, I looked forward to receiving a paycheck, but what I really enjoyed were the clients calling to thank me for a job well done. I was proud when I received referral calls because clients referred me to others with their highest recommendations.

With all the business books I've read (many of which I list in the last chapter), seminars I've attended and direct business experience I've had, I've discovered that the key to success is completely understanding and embracing the following belief: Business is not about making money. It is about serving clients' needs. When you properly serve your clients' needs, your profits soar.

It's just that simple. When all your daily thoughts and actions reflect a desire to exceed clients' needs, you will have more success than you can dream of, greater satisfaction and fulfillment in your work, and greater profitability.

Lots of books and seminars try to teach businesspeople dialogues: "When a client says this, you say that." I have two concerns about this approach. Inevitably, a client will say something for which you have no prepared response. Then what do you say? "Hang on, let me check my dialogue book"?

More important, I have great faith in people's abilities. You don't need to give people dialogue they can parrot back to make a sale or build a relationship. Given the proper training and encouragement, if they have the proper spirit of service, businesspeople will come up with better answers for clients.

Business success should not be measured only in profits.

If a manager instills the spirit of service in his or her staff, they will instinctively know how to best serve clients. Everyone wins. Clients win because they're served properly. Associates win because they have an opportunity to exercise their talent and find fulfillment in their work. And managers win because both parties are happy and things are running smoothly.

Having said this, let's broaden the definition of business success.

QUESTIONS FOR YOU

- *Do you currently find joy and satisfaction in your work?*
- *Are you more concerned with profits or with lifetime client relationships?*
- *Are you measuring your success by profits alone?*

TRUE STORY: How Do You Define Business Success?

A Washington., D.C.–area real estate company ran the following advertisement in the business section of the newspaper:

The number one real estate company in Washington, D.C., wishes to:

Thank our agents, their families, our

> *customers, and clients for making the first six months of 1999 the most successful in our history!*
>
> *Congratulations and special recognition to our Georgetown office for achieving a record breaking $61 million in sales for the month of June.*

When you focus exclusively on profit you blind yourself to larger opportunities.

First, who defines this company as "number one"? And what does "number one" refer to? Does the real estate council name it number one? Do its sales place it number one? If so, shouldn't it more accurately claim, "number one in sales"?

Further just because a company is number one in sales volume, does that automatically mean that you, as a potential client, want to do business with it? You could argue that the firm might have too much business. If you were to list or buy a home with it, you could be lost in the shuffle. Following this line of thinking, you may want to pursue another firm that isn't as busy and may be better able to devote more of its time to your needs.

Back to the text of the advertisement, what defines the "most successful year in company history"? Is it sales volume? Is it profit margin? Is it percentage of repeat and referral business? Is it the highest possible rating on a client-satisfaction survey? Is it the quality of the transaction? What if real estate firms measured and shared the percentage of sales that occurred at the original listing price of a home? Or if they measured the number of days it took for clients to find a new home or sell an existing home? In short, if this company truly did measure its success this completely and by more client-oriented indicators, how much more successful and profitable would it be?

Lastly, notice the order of whom the company

thanks. Customers and clients are last. Why is this? Doesn't the company need the clients in the first place to be in business? Don't the clients' fees pay everyone's salary? By the way, what is the difference between a customer and client? Which do you think gives this firm a better chance of earning repeat sales/listings—calling the people it serves customers, or calling them clients?

The broader your definition of business success, the greater your success and profit.

To achieve greater success, broaden your definition of success.

Redefining Business Success

As the above story points out, most businesses measure their success strictly by their own standards, in terms of sales volume, profit margins or stockholder return. Our business society constantly reinforces this view. Books of business lists abound, telling us that the most successful companies are those with the highest revenues or the highest shareholder return. This is an extremely limited and short-sighted way to measure business success. It does not take into account any measure of client satisfaction, quality of work or service, repeat and referral business, or longevity in business. Bigger does not always mean better.

In my early years in business, I too fell for this myth. I measured my success strictly by my own sales volume: What total dollar amount did I sell? Then, as I sold more, I added profitability to my success measurement. I measured not just what I sold, but the profit the company made. I was getting a little wiser, but not much.

With 20 years of seasoned business experience, I've broadened and reordered my goals for achieving long-term business success and satisfaction. In a funny twist, what was once first, increasing sales volume, became last.

It may have been acceptable in the past to measure success by your own standards. However, in today's fiercely competitive business environment, to be truly successful and profitable you must broaden your definition of business success. No longer can you gauge success strictly by sales, profit or shareholder return. If you want to survive and thrive in this new century, you should include measurements that are important to your clients.

Treat each client interaction as if it's your last opportunity to serve your client.

No matter where you work in an organization, when you want to be successful, recognize that true business success encompasses the following components and in this order:

1. Exceeding clients' expectations. This means exceeding the client's expectations, not yours, consistently on each project. No matter where you work in an organization, you always have an opportunity to exceed a client's expectation. You can answer the telephone more quickly. You can be more polite. You can go out of your way to make sure clients are taken care of. In short, in your clients' eyes, your service should be a 10 out of a possible score of 10.

2. Receiving glowing client testimonials. Besides dollars, we need another measure of business success. Client letters, received from people who are so impressed with your work that they are moved to write testimonials, are an excellent indicator. How do you get clients to write glowing letters about your service? Read number three below.

The best time to ask for a testimonial letter is when clients gush over your work. At that point, thank them for their kind words and ask them if they would put their praise in writing and send it to you. Then include these letters in all your proposals. Make sure all your prospective clients see the words of praise from your existing clients. The most effective way to sell prospective clients is through the words of existing clients.

The most effective way to gain new clients is through the word of existing clients.

3. Earning a client for life. Do such outstanding work that you earn a client for life. Clients will be so wowed by you and your service that you are guaranteed their business for life.

4. Earning referral sales. Clients should be so impressed with your work that they not only refer you to others, but they speak so glowingly about you that they make the sale for you. When you're really on top of your game, you won't have to ask for referrals. They'll come naturally.

5. Increasing profitability. By focusing on all the preceding goals, you will achieve greater profitability for two reasons: You decrease costs by doing a job right the first time, and you save money because you don't have to advertise for clients. To achieve number one through four above, you have to continually improve and refine your business systems. When you do this, clients will come back again and again. You don't have to spend valuable resources attracting new clients—they will be chasing you!

6. Increasing sales volume. This is the natural result of doing things right and in the right order. You achieve increased sales not by aiming for them but by accomplishing all of the above.

In short, if you are measuring your "success" only on the basis of sales volume and profit, you are not getting a complete and accurate picture of your company's performance. It is your view of success, not your client's.

Measure your success by what's important to your clients.

What had been my number-one criterion of success in my less experienced days—increased sales volume—fell to last place. However, I quickly learned that all the criteria for earning repeat and referral business contributed to increased sales. Anyone can lie, steal, cheat, pillage or plunder for the order; it is the lifetime relationship you want to gain.

I achieved increased sales volume not by focusing on achieving it but by focusing on continually improving my services and exceeding my clients' expectations. When I focused on exceeding clients' expectations, the increased sales volume came naturally, as did long-term profitability. Most businesses fail to recognize or understand that profit is the by-product of doing outstanding work, not the goal.

QUESTIONS FOR YOU

- *Do you measure your clients' satisfaction on a daily basis? How? What feedback system do you have to measure it?*
- *When did you last receive a positive client letter? What do you do with them? Do you show them to prospective clients?*
- *How do you measure the quality of your work?*
- *Do you measure repeat business?*
- *Do you properly thank your clients for their repeat business? How?*
- *Do you measure referral business?*

- *How do you thank clients for the referral business they send you?*
- *Whose view of success is more important, yours or your client's?*
- *Do you measure complete business success by the six criteria above?*

Serve rather than sell.

TRUE STORY: Johnson & Johnson: Dedicated to Exceeding Clients' Expectations

Perhaps you are reading along and thinking, "This putting clients first is pretty Pollyanna-ish. It might work for small- to medium-size businesses, but can it help a Fortune 500 company?"

This strategy of putting clients first is not restricted to small businesses. It can be used successfully in large corporations. What I mean by "successfully" is that everyone wins—clients, associates and stockholders—and the company earns record profits. Let's share a real-life example.

In 1994, Johnson & Johnson enjoyed annual sales of $15.7 billion. It earned a net profit of $2 billion. Most companies would die for $15.7 billion in yearly sales, which is indeed impressive. However, what is more impressive is the $2 billion profit. You could sell $1 million a year and have costs of $999,999 to get those sales. All you earn is a dollar. Some businesses have costs that exceed their sales. It's not what you sell, it's the profit you make that ultimately matters.

Further, Johnson & Johnson has made a profit every year since 1944, which is virtually unheard of on Wall Street. Most companies have years of gains followed by years of loss, an up-and-down

THE JOHNSON & JOHNSON CREDO

We believe our first responsibility is to the doctors, nurses and patients, to mothers and fathers and all others who use our products and services. In meeting their needs everything we do must be of high quality. We must constantly strive to reduce our costs in order to maintain reasonable prices. Customers' orders must be serviced promptly and accurately. Our suppliers and distributors must have an opportunity to make a fair profit.

We are responsible to our employees, the men and women who work with us throughout the world. Everyone must be considered as an individual. We must respect their dignity and recognize their merit. They must have a sense of security in their jobs. Compensation must be fair and adequate, and working conditions clean, orderly and safe. We must be mindful of ways to help our employees fulfill their family responsibilities. Employees must feel free to make suggestions and complaints. There must be equal opportunity for employment, development and advancement for those qualified. We must provide competent management, and their actions must be just and ethical.

We are responsible to the communities in which we live and work and to the world community as well. We must be good citizens—support good works and charities and bear our fair share of taxes. We must encourage civic improvements and better health and education. We must maintain in good order the property we are privileged to use, protecting the environment and natural resources.

Our final responsibility is to our stockholders. Business must make a sound profit. We must experiment with new ideas. Research must be carried on, innovative programs developed and mistakes paid for. New equipment must be purchased, new facilities provided and new products launched. Reserves must be created to provide for adverse times. When we operate according to these principles, the stockholders should realize a fair return.

The Johnson & Johnson Credo is reprinted with permission from Johnson & Johnson.

cycle over which the company has little control. Johnson & Johnson has made money every single year since it has been a public company.

What is even more remarkable is that Johnson & Johnson is the parent company of McNeil–PPC Inc., which makes Tylenol™. Remember the two disasters in the 1980s related to Tylenol™? Tylenol™ capsules were linked to a total of eight deaths, seven in Chicago in 1982 and one in New York City in 1986. Take a second and think about this. What worse fate could befall a company that produces health products? No matter what field of business you are in, you will be hard pressed to find a greater challenge.

If you have a credo, live the words daily. If not, then write a credo.

Even with all the trouble it went through, including voluntarily pulling Tylenol™ from all store shelves, Johnson & Johnson still made enough money in those years to turn a profit. Not only that, Johnson & Johnson weathered the storms, and Tylenol™ has earned even greater market share after the crises.

What accounts for this incredible earnings track record and the resilience of the company? Why is Johnson & Johnson so successful? Part of the answer lies in the company's credo. I have reprinted the Johnson & Johnson Credo in its entirety on page 80.

The Johnson & Johnson Credo

Three things are important about the Johnson & Johnson Credo:

1. The son of one of the founders of Johnson & Johnson felt having a credo was important. R.W. Johnson Jr. took the time to put into writing what was important to him in conducting business.

Because Johnson & Johnson has a credo, everyone in the company clearly understands where the firm is headed. The company's priorities are clear for everyone—associates, clients, prospective clients and stockholders—to see. Don't underestimate the importance of this. If a question ever arises about policy, the staff consults the credo. It's a guiding light, a beacon that directs them to the right course of action.

Make your clients your first priority, stockholders your last.

In an interesting note, before the Tylenol™ crises, Johnson & Johnson had considered eliminating the credo. James Burke, CEO at the time, thought it had become outdated and went so far as to send out a memo to that effect. The credo issue was sidetracked by the Tylenol™ crises. After the crises, Burke and others at Johnson & Johnson credited the credo for guiding them through one of the most challenging times in company history. They had dealt with the crises by following the credo. Instead of being eliminated, the credo became further entrenched at Johnson & Johnson.

2. The credo is all about service. The first sentence clearly states Johnson & Johnson's first priority. I think it's one of the most important lines in the business history of the 20th century. It focuses on clients and service: "We believe our first responsibility is to the doctors, nurses and patients, to mothers and fathers and all others who use our products and services." It doesn't get much clearer than that: We are in business to serve our clients.

Now go back and review Johnson & Johnson's annual sales figures and its profits, and remember that it has made money every year since it became a public company—not most years, but every year. Do you see a correlation between this credo of service and Johnson & Johnson's performance?

3. The company makes its clients its first priority. The last paragraph, not the first, mentions stockholders. The company's last responsibility is to its stockholders. Johnson & Johnson doesn't put the cart before the horse. It isn't so obsessed with profits that it forgets its clients. In fact, Johnson & Johnson recognizes how important it is to serve its clients first, then earn a sound profit.

In short, Johnson & Johnson's credo says, "Let's take care of our clients, our co-workers, our managers and our communities, and the money will follow." The proof is in the pudding. Johnson & Johnson has earned a profit year after year.

Print across your paychecks: "Funded by our clients."

QUESTIONS FOR YOU

- *Do you have a company credo?*
- *Have you clearly communicated your company's priorities and objectives to your clients, associates and stockholders?*
- *If you do not have a company credo and decided to write one, what would it say?*
- *What's your first priority?*
- *To whom is your first responsibility?*

Actions Matching Words

One danger of having a credo is that it can become just words on a page. The words of a company's credo and the actions of the company must match The time you spend to put together a credo doesn't matter if its words aren't followed. Johnson & Johnson does live its credo.

When the Tylenol™ crises occurred, Johnson & Johnson voluntarily withdrew Tylenol™ capsules from shelves all over the world. Instead of waiting until it was forced to do so by the government or public opinion, the company took decisive action on its own.

Yes, pulling the capsules cost a pretty penny, but Johnson & Johnson was living up to the opening words of the credo: Its first responsibility was to serving its clients. If the company had not voluntarily pulled the capsules, it would not have been living up to its credo.

Don't be obsessed with profits. Be posessed with quality and client service. Profits will follow.

Given the choice between maximizing profit in the short term and protecting clients, Johnson & Johnson chose to protect its clients. Because it took this step, it ensured long-term profitability. Maybe that's why Tylenol™ has greater market share today than it did before the crises.

When you want to be successful—find greater fulfillment in your work, gain more lifetime clients and earn greater profits—put your clients first.

Lifetime Tool 3 is to focus on the needs of your clients first and work on developing a lifetime client relationship. Be in business for your clients and, in measuring your success, include indicators that are important to your clients.

QUESTION FOR YOU

- *Do your company's words and actions match?*

THINGS TO DO "MONDAY MORNING"

- **Chase the client, not the dollar.**
- **Serve client needs first.** Build lifetime client relationships, and profitability will follow.
- **Every single action you take** should be in your clients' best interests.
- **Measure your success** by what's important to your clients.
- **Live up to your clients' expectations of you.**

Superserving Your Clients

LIFETIME TOOL

4

CUSTOMER ONCE, CLIENT FOREVER

In this chapter, I'll share:

- **How to bring greater value to clients**
- **How to form even stronger client relationships**
- **The importance of good manners in business**

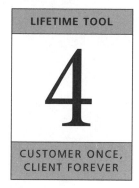

In today's fiercely competitive business environment, it's not enough to properly serve clients' needs. You need to go further. You need to do all you can to become an indispensable resource to your clients. You need to help clients be more successful and profitable. This chapter will offer strategies to accomplish this.

Superserve Your Clients

To help clients become more profitable and successful, you must "superserve" them. This means going above and beyond the normal call of service—going beyond what a client would reasonably expect. In a client's world, you bring added value. Superserving means truly making clients' jobs easier. Here are examples of two businesspeople who superserve their clients. (Author's note: I am grateful to Fred Robinson for introducing to me the term "superserving.")

TRUE STORY: Tom Folkert Goes the Extra Mile

Tom Folkert, a regional marketing manager for Monumental Life Insurance, sells preneed insurance to funeral directors. He has approximately 100 accounts throughout the southwestern U.S.

I recently read Tom's business plan for the upcoming year and saw that it demonstrated two excellent examples of superserving clients. In the first example, one of Tom's clients was looking for a marketing director. Tom saw an opportunity to build a stronger bond with a client, and he took the initiative. Tom sat down with this client and together they developed the job requirements of this position. Then, he went a step further and helped his client locate the right marketing person.

Do all you can to make your clients' jobs easier; always look for more ways to serve them.

In the second example, Tom had another client who wanted to sell his funeral home. Having recently helped another owner find a buyer for his funeral home, Tom became actively involved in locating a prospective buyer for this client.

Nowhere in Tom's job description does it call for him to help clients write job descriptions or locate prospective buyers for a firm. Tom, however, is a seasoned businessperson. He knows that when he does this type of work he will develop lifetime bonds with his clients. When these clients need service, who is the first person they will call? Who helped them in the past? Who served as a trusted adviser? All Tom's time and energy are investments that will pay handsome dividends.

QUESTION FOR YOU

- *How are you superserving your clients?*

TRUE STORY: Carl Sewell's Cadillac Dealership—Client Retention in Action

Sometimes superserving means you spend or invest a little money to gain a lot of loyalty, as in this story.

Carl Sewell, author of *Customers for Life,* believes so much in retaining his existing clients that Sewell Cadillac will at any hour of the day send one of its trucks out to replace a broken key at no charge. Now take a moment and think about this. It may cost the dealership a couple hundred dollars by the time all is said and done to send a man out to Dallas–Fort Worth airport at 2 A.M. to replace a broken car key.

Be readily accessible to your clients.

If Carl's dealerships do this two or three times a month, how many of these grateful clients do you think will make it a point to have their cars serviced by Carl, and/or will return to buy another car from Carl? More important, how many other potential clients will they tell about this positive experience?

If just one client returns, or sends Carl one referral sale, the dealership will recoup its investment. Think of all the free advertising Carl's dealership is earning as a result of this service. After all, aren't you reading about it right now?

QUESTIONS FOR YOU

- *When did you last receive service like this?*
- *How did it make you feel?*
- *How many people did you tell about it?*
- *Are you going the extra mile, like Monumental Life and Sewell Cadillac, by superserving your clients?*

Why Staying in Touch With Clients Is So Important

One simple way to superserve clients is to anticipate their needs and call them before they have to call you—which may mean tracking down your telephone number, hearing your phone ring six times before someone answers, and learning that you're out. Be readily accessible to your clients.

I recently conducted a customer service training program for a waste-management company, in whose industry competition for clients is fierce. One of the customer service representatives, Jenny, told the story of losing a client to a competitor because the competitor offered a lower price.

To keep clients, stay in touch with them.

Jenny had developed enough rapport with the client that she felt comfortable asking if she could follow up with him in a couple of months to check on his new service and be sure that his needs were being met. In effect, she was superserving the client.

About two weeks later, before Jenny had the opportunity to call him, the client called her and said he was disgusted with the competitor's service and wanted to restart with her firm.

Jenny did a wonderful job of laying the proper groundwork and developing the rapport so the client could return. The company had 12 customer service representatives. What if all 12 could bring in an additional client a month?

Here are some additional strategies to superserve clients:

Call a client and check in just to say hello. See how business is. Ask how you can help the client be more successful. What challenges is he or she facing that you can assist with? Ask clients how you can bring them greater value. Depending on your client's needs, stay in touch every four to six weeks. Preprogram your contact-management system (ACT, Gold-mine or Maximizer, for instance) to prompt you to touch base with your clients.

Read as many newspapers and publications as

possible and send pertinent articles to your clients. Send clients suggestions on how they can be more successful. Have lunch with clients to figure out how you can help them be more successful and profitable.

Keep your eyes open to other resources that can assist your clients. When you are out in the business world, keep your eyes and ears open to other resources or opportunities for your clients. For instance, if you have a client who is a printer and in your travels you learn of a request for printing bids, call your client and make him aware of it.

Think of yourself as an unofficial member of your clients' staff.

Keep your ears open for any business opportunities for your clients. Either bring your clients business or introduce them to other potential sources of income in their line of business. Make sure your clients are aware of all possible business opportunities. Don't automatically assume they know about the business. Do whatever you can to make your clients' jobs easier and help them to be more successful.

Obviously, the better you understand your clients' business and their needs, the better you can serve them.

QUESTIONS FOR YOU

- *Are you leaving the door open for clients to call you when they are unhappy with a competitor's service?*
- *Are you making it easy for your clients to return by staying in touch?*
- *Are you superserving clients by supplying pertinent information and helpful leads?*
- *What opportunities do you have to superserve your clients by improved communication?*

The Importance of Good Manners

One last point on superserving clients: Exhibit your best manners with your clients. Unfortunately, in business today it's the exception to the rule when a businessperson treats a client with good manners. Think about it: When was the last time a businessperson wowed you with courtesy and hospitality?

Always be polite to your clients.

It costs nothing to provide clients with good manners. Savvy businesspeople use good manners because they know it helps them win and maximize a relationship. I suggest you practice good manners because you recognize that without clients, you would not be in business.

Tim Schilling is president of Early, Cassidy & Schilling, an insurance agency in Gaithersburg, Md. I have a friend who is a client of Tim's. This gentleman has been in business for more than 40 years. Whenever he speaks of Tim, he always comments that after every meeting, Tim shakes his hand, looks him in the eye and thanks him for his business.

Are you properly thanking clients for the opportunity to serve them? For your reference, I have included (on pages 92 and 93) two of the best thank-you notes I have received over the years.

Let me make two quick comments on these thank-you notes:

1. Both letters immediately thank me for shopping at their establishments. I especially like the R & M Sports letter, "Thank you for allowing us to do business with you." Also, both letters remind me that the stores "can serve you in the future."

2. Notice how the notes are personalized. They are handwritten and both salespeople knew enough about the purchases to make a comment in the letter.

QUESTION FOR YOU

- *Are you writing thank-you letters to your clients?*

Always Be Polite, Kind and Generous to Your Clients

Always treat your clients as you would like to be treated.

You don't have to superserve clients to be polite to them. This is a good opportunity to offer some additional suggestions on how to properly treat clients.

I have sat in the lobbies of client offices and watched polite salespeople treated to a cup of coffee and led into their meetings by a smiling receptionist. Conversely, I have seen rude salespeople be told that their prospective client is "unavailable" and that they should try back another time.

When you want to develop lifetime clients, display manners that reflect that desire. I can't emphasize enough the importance of being polite to clients and putting their concerns ahead of yours. Here's a suggested list of proper manners to use when dealing with clients:

Let clients speak first. Don't interrupt. Let your clients finish expressing their thoughts. Think about what a client has just tried to convey to you before you speak.

Call clients before they have to track down your telephone number and call you. If you can't reach

LETTER FROM R&M SPORTING GOODS

R & M Sporting Goods
112 Citadel Mall
Charleston, SC 29407

5/4/96

Mr. Buckingham,

Thank you for calling us and allowing us to do business with you. We hope the boys enjoy the raft you sent them. Please let us know when we can serve you in the future.

Thank you again for your business.

Sincerely,

Michael & the employees of Resorting to Sports

LETTER FROM HERMES

HERMÈS

14 February 1997

Dear Mr Buckingham,

I want to thankyou for your visit to our boutique. I was a pleasure meeting you and helping you with your gifts.

I am sure the scarves will be received with much enthusiasm. The green 'Jumping' scarf is beautiful and that shade of green is very popular now, and the 'chantilly' pochette is great for wearing or framing.

Please let me know if I can ever be of any assistance. Take care and once again, many thanks.

Sincerely,

Jamie Rosas

FAIRFAX SQUARE AT TYSONS CORNER
8075 LEESBURG PIKE • VIENNA, VIRGINIA 22182
TEL (703) 506-4546 • FAX (703) 506-4593

them, leave a detailed voice message with clear instructions about how and when they can reach you. Always leave your telephone number.

Return all client telephone calls the same day. The last thing you want is for clients to feel that their calls are lost in the great void of voice mail.

Listen, take notes as you talk with clients, and interweave their words and phrases into your responses.

If you do not reach a client, leave a message. Let the client know you were trying to get in touch with him or her. Always leave your telephone number even if the person taking the message says he or she already has it. Also leave a couple of convenient times for the client to reach you. If you really want to be on top of your game, don't let clients track you down. Keep calling them until you reach them.

Don't ask clients to call you. Be easy to do business with. You should always initiate contact. Don't make your clients have to track you down.

Be on time for your appointments! Don't keep clients waiting. If you are not going to be on time, call clients and let them know. When you see the client, apologize for being late.

Do not take other telephone calls when you are speaking with a client. Do not put a client on hold to take someone else's call. Finish with one client before you get involved with someone else.

If your pager goes off, don't read it in front of a client. If you have to read it, ask your client's permission: "I am expecting an important page. Do you mind if I read my pager?"

Turn off your cellular telephone when you are with a client. Focus on the client with whom you're meeting.

Be immediately reachable to all your clients. Clients should not have to wait more than three hours for you to get back to them.

Practice good manners. Be as polite as you can be to clients. After all, they pay our salaries. I have found success addressing clients as "Mr." and "Ms."

In short, the more pleasant you are to do business with, the sooner clients will return and refer others to you.

After an important meeting, send a letter to your client summarizing key issues.

TRUE STORY: Soothing an Angry Client

I have a good friend, Douglas, who is extremely particular about customer service. If you ever want someone to critique your customer service department, he's your man.

Douglas had leased a car he was not happy with. He was unhappy with both the car and the service he received at the dealership. One thing led to another until, finally, he had had enough. (The last straw was when the dealership sold off the line of car Douglas had leased.)

He called the president of the dealership, and when he did not receive a return call within 24 hours, he prepared a searing letter. He sent me the letter to review before sending it to the dealership.

I told him the letter had too much emotion and not enough facts. But before he could revise and mail the letter, the president of the dealership called him. Douglas said he would like to meet him. Douglas called me excitedly to tell me of the meeting. He was going to set the dealership straight. He told me he would call me afterward.

After his meeting Douglas called me, and the roaring lion was now a meek lamb. His voice, once loud and indignant, was quiet and humble.

Good manners help defuse clients' anger.

Douglas told me that the president of the dealership could not have been nicer. He treated Douglas like his number-one client. He welcomed Douglas into his office and during the entire meeting addressed him as "Mr.," although he was twice Douglas's age. The president patiently listened to all of Douglas's concerns. Then he explained the entire situation. While he was not able to meet Douglas's request, he offered an alternative. How could Douglas still be upset?

My friend's anger was neutralized by the president's good manners. The moral of the story is that politeness and kind manners can do much to quell clients' anger and build better rapport.

QUESTION FOR YOU

- *Are you properly dealing with angry clients?*

THINGS TO DO "MONDAY MORNING"

- **Become an indispensable resource to your clients.** Do whatever you can to make your clients more successful and profitable.
- **Call clients before they call you;** anticipate client needs.
- **Maintain a meaningful dialogue with clients.** Always ask how you can serve them.
- **Remember to thank clients for the opportunity to serve them.**

Building Lifetime Client Rapport

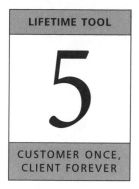

LIFETIME TOOL

5

CUSTOMER ONCE, CLIENT FOREVER

In this chapter, I'll share:

- **Fourteen strategies for building lifetime client rapport**
- **How to find common ground with clients**

The stronger your relationship with your client, the greater your opportunity for additional business. However, your time in front of a client is extremely short. You don't have much of an opportunity to make a winning impression. The first step to building trust is to develop rapport, which, simply defined, is a harmonious and sympathetic relationship.

In this chapter, I share strategies you can use every day to build greater rapport, trust, and, ultimately, a stronger lifetime relationship with your clients. While people in technical support and customer service positions will find these strategies particularly useful, you will benefit from them no matter what your role is in your company.

Rapport-Building Strategies

When I first started in business, I had no concept of how valuable my time in front of a client was. I had no idea of the important information I could learn or the rapport and trust I could develop in such a short period of time. Over the years, I've grown a lot wiser. I've watched excellent businesspeople begin to develop outstanding rapport in the first five minutes of a client meeting. You may have only 15 minutes face to face with a client. Are you using your time wisely?

This chapter came about because of a response I received at a workshop years ago. The workshop was presented to a media sales team. On the GoalStar feedback questionnaire, I asked what issues I could present in future workshops to help people become more successful.

Tear down the walls of client distrust.

One person answered, "Help us tear down the walls between us and our clients." I liked her idea of trying to get closer to clients, so I developed a section on how to build lifetime client rapport. Relationships with clients can't last a lifetime if you don't have rapport for a lifetime. To have such rapport, we have to tear down walls of distrust.

It's not enough to be aware of the rapport-building strategies I describe. I'm sure you're familiar with some of the strategies in this chapter. The opportunity is in their constant application. To develop and maintain lifetime clients, you must constantly be aware of these strategies and apply them in all your interactions with your clients.

Please understand that these strategies do not constitute a shortcut or a quick lesson in how to schmooze people. Lots of books take that approach. The point is not to be able to chat nicely with clients, but rather to be able to build lifetime rapport.

1. Smile, Smile, Smile

I know it's simple, but are you doing it consistently? This is not just to look good in front of your prospective client; you want to be at ease and comfortable with yourself. In addition, you want to put your client at ease. To smile, think about the positive aspects of doing business with your client—why you're in business in the first place. Remember all the value you bring to a client. The more you show your enjoyment in the relationship, the more at ease and comfortable your client will be. To build a lifetime partnership, start off on the right foot.

TRUE STORY: Why Smiling on the Telephone Is So Important

Build lifelong client rapport through real conversation, not small talk.

I once did a workshop for a public relations firm and mentioned the importance of smiling. The firm has 10 to 12 people who spend all day on the telephone booking appointments. When I mentioned how important it is to smile, one woman, with a smile, raised her hand and shared with the group her approach: She keeps a mirror at her desk, and before she makes any client calls, she makes sure she is smiling. Guess who consistently booked the most appointments?

It is important to recognize just how crucial it is to smile over the telephone. Clients can't see your smile, but they can "hear" your smile.

QUESTION FOR YOU

- *Are you smiling when you're with your clients?*

2. Genuinely Compliment Your Clients

I am surprised at how few businesspeople do this consistently. Note that I use the word "genuinely." If you can't genuinely compliment a client, don't bother trying. Nothing kills rapport more quickly than a phony compliment.

For example, if your prospective client has had a great deal of business success, compliment her on that. When appropriate, take notice of and compliment clients on their clothing. Be sure to keep such comments light and devoid of any sexual innuendo. Take note of your client's office—comment on the view, or how well-designed the office is. Notice any awards or pictures that you can comment on.

Always be sincere and begin conversations by genuinely complimenting clients.

Your compliment does not have to be based on external appearances. If you notice that a client has done a good deal of research, compliment him or her on that. When I get into a business discussion, I always make sure to acknowledge that a client has made a good point, even if that point may appear to run counter to what I am saying. If you can't find anything to compliment your clients on, simply thank them for the time they are taking with you.

For those of you who play golf, complimenting a client at the outset of an appointment is the equivalent of hitting a drive 250 yards down the center of the fairway. You're off to a great start, setting yourself up for a successful conversation. In addition, this habit encourages you to look for the positive in people, which will enable you to better enjoy your work—and the rest of your life.

QUESTION FOR YOU

- *When was the last time you genuinely complimented a client?*

3. Take a Genuine Interest in Your Clients

I again stress the word "genuine." Most people see through feigned interest, and when they do, you'll fail to built the rapport you desire.

One of the things I enjoy most about business is the variety of people I meet in the course of an average day. One minute I'm talking to a manager or owner, the next I'm working with a salesperson, a customer service representative or a field engineer. All these people have different interests.

I look forward to drawing people out and learning about their interests. At the appropriate time, strike up a conversation with clients about their hobbies, family, friends, schools, where they live, what sports teams they like, how they spend their free time. I always like to find out how and why people got into the line of work they are in. The trick here is to let the conversation be driven by your clients' interests.

Take a personal interest in your clients.

TRUE STORY: Rewards in Commonality

Four years ago, I conducted a workshop for an engineering firm. The branch manager, Matt, told a great story of winning an account after years of no success.

Having no luck trying to sell the account over the telephone, Matt decided to go see the client, which is always a good idea. When he arrived at the client's office, he got sidetracked by a car in the parking lot with a Clemson University sticker. Matt went to Clemson, and to say he is a Clemson fan would be a drastic understatement. Matt eats, drinks and sleeps Clemson.

Forgetting his appointment, Matt began to focus on finding out who went to Clemson. When he went into the office, instead of asking for his appointment, he asked who went to Clemson. Guess who went to Clemson? The guy Matt had been trying to sell to for all these years! It turned out Matt's potential client was a bigger Clemson fan than Matt!

Thirty minutes later, after they had exchanged Clemson stories and bonded, Matt and his client began to talk business. Not only did he get the project, he also won the account. How could he not?

4. Find Commonality

Look for the best in your clients—it's more enjoyable.

Even before I meet with a client, I'm looking for common ground. If it's a referral call, I try to learn as much as I can from my referral source about the client's interests. What is the prospective client like? What interests does he have? Where is he from? Where did he go to school? I focus on a common point.

An easy way to find commonality is to do as I suggested above and look at pictures, awards or diplomas in clients' offices to see if they suggest shared interests. You might find that your prospective client is as big a baseball, golf or football fan as you are, or went to the same school as you or someone else you know. The person may enjoy the same art, politics, books, places or foods you do. He or she may have twins like you. Set yourself up to win by starting your conversation with that point of common ground.

If you don't feel that interested in other people's lives, work on taking an interest. You might find that people begin to take more interest in you. While you are finding out about clients' business needs, find out about them personally, too. You'll find the results rewarding no matter how much profit you generate.

To break the ice in developing client relationships, here are some typical questions that you can ask clients:

- **What do you do in your spare time?**
- **What are your hobbies?**

- **What did you do over the weekend?**
- **Where are you from?**
- **Where did you go to school?**
- **What does your spouse or significant other do for a living?**

Be sure to avoid sounding as if you're interrogating your clients for information. This is not a script. Your questions should come up naturally in the conversation. Let your conversation be interest-driven. An outstanding resource for additional client questions is the "MacKay 66"—a set of 66 excellent questions to ask clients found in Harvey MacKay's informative book *Swim With the Sharks*.

Treat everyone like a potential client.

I find it's always a good idea to leave a conversation with an item you can use to begin a future conversation. It might be sports, business, current events, family, friends, children, movies, sailing, travel, or anything that is appropriate to your client.

QUESTIONS FOR YOU

- *Are you learning about your clients' interests?*
- *Are you finding common ground with clients?*

5. Listen Carefully

Another strategy to develop rapport with clients is to listen completely, to give them your total undivided attention. As I suggested in the last chapter, focus entirely on your clients. Avoid interruptions and distractions like telephone calls, pagers, people knocking on the door, open doors and ringing telephones. Make your clients feel as if they are the center of your universe.

If clients are in your office, close the door, hold your telephone calls and turn off all pagers, beepers and cell phones. Let them know that they have your complete attention. If you ever doubt the importance and value of giving clients your undivided attention, think about the last person who gave you his or her undivided attention and remember how you felt.

You not only need to listen to what your clients are saying, you need to listen actively. Active listening means paying attention, asking questions, restating the message to make sure you understand what the clients are saying, and looking and listening for the emotions behind the words. The concept of active listening is so important that I devote the next chapter to it.

Listen carefully by giving your clients your undivided attention.

In addition, you need to recognize that most clients don't know exactly what they want. They have a vague idea but aren't entirely sure. Most other businesspeople care only about making money and not about completely understanding the true needs of their clients. They don't take the time to learn what clients' true needs are—to really listen to them.

In business, and especially in sales, when you listen well both parties jointly discover clients' needs. In identifying and subsequently addressing these needs, you begin to develop the lifetime relationship.

To become a better listener, focus on how much you talk and how much your clients talk. Listen from your clients' perspectives. Who's doing most of the talking? Are your clients getting a chance to make their points?

Monitor just how carefully you're listening. Taking notes and maintaining eye contact are two excellent strategies with which to begin improving listening skills.

Asking the right questions to discover your clients' real needs is also critical, so I devote another chapter to that tool (Lifetime Tool 7). Read the following two chapters for more tips on active listening and on asking the right questions.

QUESTIONS FOR YOU

- *What client relationships will you significantly improve by giving your clients your undivided attention?*
- *Said another way, how much more repeat and referral business will you receive from clients when you give them your undivided attention?*
- *On a scale of 1 to 10, how effective are you as a listener?*
- *How would your clients rate you?*

Help your clients recognize and verbalize their needs.

6. Speak Your Client's Language

I have watched many businesspeople try to impress clients by using the fancy jargon of their own industry, not necessarily the language their clients use and understand. While these people think they are impressing their clients, they're actually confusing them or, worse yet, making them feel ignorant.

At the same time, I've seen businesspeople who haven't bothered to learn anything about their clients' businesses and thus constantly show their own ignorance and lack of interest every time they speak.

Both of these scenarios are especially apt to occur when businesspeople or their clients have highly technical areas of expertise—in fields such as information technology or law—that are prone to jargon.

I have found success by starting at square one with clients. Assume your clients know very little about what you do. Use clear and simple language to express what you have to offer. Don't be afraid to ask questions if you don't understand some area of their business. Use analogies to their business to relate what you're offering to what they do every day and to their specific needs.

Know when to speak plain English and when to use "technospeak."

If both you and your client are in the same field, or at least share expertise on the product you are offering, you can more freely use the specialized language and jargon of that field. Still, however, ask questions that will assure you that your clients understand what you are saying.

And don't get left behind in a storm of jargon delivered by your clients. Instead of feigning understanding, ask questions for clarification, even at the risk of appearing ignorant. You can't truly serve your clients' needs if you don't understand them.

TRUE STORY: Suit Your Language to the Client

John Phillips, president of a successful computer-service company that I work with, has many strengths in business. Perhaps his greatest strength is his ability to relate to people in the language they understand. In an industry notorious for people who try to impress you with jargon and who have a difficult time relating to clients, Phillips patiently listens to his clients and explains computer solutions in understandable language.

Phillips relates to people at their level. When he is in the field providing technical support with well-versed personnel, he speaks in the language of the most current trade journal. When he meets the managing partner of a law firm who knows nothing about computers, he speaks about computers in a language that the partner understands. Because

Phillips determines people's degree of computer knowledge and competency and relates to them on that level, he enjoys much business success.

QUESTION FOR YOU

- *Are you speaking your clients' language—so they understand you and you understand them?*

7. Don't Immediately Disagree With Clients

Focus on where you agree with your clients.

Besides feigning interest or being phony, another way for you to kill rapport is to immediately disagree with a client or to appear argumentative. While agreeing with your client can be a powerful tool for building rapport, disagreeing can be an equally powerful tool for destroying rapport.

When clients say something you agree with, let them know you clearly and emphatically agree: "I couldn't agree with you more." When clients say something you may not agree with, don't disagree immediately, no matter what you think. Focus instead on where you do agree, or try to see the clients' point of view. Consider saying something like, "I agree with you that . . ." or "I can appreciate how you may feel" or "I never thought of it that way" or "That's an interesting way to look at it."

TRUE STORY: The Value of Agreeing

Years ago I met with a client who had been highly recommended and whom I had aggressively pursued for years. When I finally sat down with Mark (just getting a face-to-face meeting was a victory), the first thing he said was that he did not like professional speakers. Maybe that's why he didn't respond to all my "marketing efforts." Mark told me that he felt talk was cheap, and that all speakers did was talk. Action, he felt, was what ultimately mattered.

When I was younger and less experienced, I might have taken issue with Mark. Before our meeting had even gotten started, I might have tried to argue that speakers are valuable.

Argue the point, not the person.

It just so happened that I believe some of what Mark said, and I told him so. I focused on where we agreed. It may very well have surprised Mark that I tended to agree with him and told him why. Then I explained how I thought my programs were different from those of other speakers.

The rest of our meeting went well. We had a pleasant hour-long discussion in which Mark gave me a much greater understanding of his company's needs—eight pages of notes' worth. I was fortunate to earn an opportunity to address his group.

I am reasonably confident that if I had taken issue with him, I never would have built enough rapport to understand his needs and probably would not have won a contract. Looking back on it, I wonder if Mark wasn't just testing me to see how I would respond.

8. Choose Your Battles

In avoiding disagreement, I am not implying that you arbitrarily agree with everything your clients say. If you do that, they will never trust your opinion. I am saying to choose your battles carefully, and choose at the right time.

When you do disagree with a client, make sure that you oppose the point, not the person. You will not build lifetime rapport with clients by making them feel that they're not intelligent or that they've made poor choices. You will build rapport by gently pointing out faulty thinking, sharing your expertise and offering creative solutions.

Your first meeting with a client is not the time to tell him that you completely disagree with his strategy. You build rapport first, focus on areas of agreement, educate your client, then suggest alternative strategies.

Avoid knee-jerk reactions. Take time to understand why clients feel the way they do.

Say, for example, that you're a financial adviser and you know that your client should do his estate planning. The client, however, wants to continue making investments and put off estate planning. You need to remind him of the urgency of estate planning. You don't tell the client he's crazy for not doing estate planning; you gently point out all the possible ramifications that might occur because of your client's procrastination.

In short, never make your clients feel that you think they don't know what they're talking about. Rapport will be built only on a foundation of mutual respect and trust.

QUESTIONS FOR YOU

- *Do you disagree with your clients too quickly—before you acknowledge the points on which you do agree?*
- *Do you insist on your point of view without hearing or respecting your clients' point of view?*

9. Learn to Read Your Clients

Always be aware of where you stand with clients. This is precisely why I offered the "Liked Best, Next Time" exercise in the very first chapter of this book (please see pages 26 to 32).

You will become much more effective in business when you develop an awareness of your skills and how you relate to people. Developing this awareness takes time.

From the minute you meet or speak with clients, be aware of what your clients are thinking about you. Are you connecting with them? Do they like you? Are you building rapport? Are you having a positive impact?

Develop an ability to read clients' intentions and motivations.

Just as an excellent public speaker reads his audience by studying their postures and facial expressions, you must read your clients when you communicate with them. Are your words resonating with your clients? Are you boring them or inspiring them?

Sharp salespeople have an easier time reading clients than do customer service people because salespeople are more likely to be face to face with their clients and can see the clients' body language. Salespeople, meeting clients in person, are following their every word and know whether clients are happy.

Most customer service people can only hear their clients. They have to rely on reading voice tone and voice speed to know what kind of impact they are having on a client.

Be aware that clients may present themselves one way in person or on the telephone and another way when they write. What are they really saying in their letters or e-mail messages? You need to ensure that you understand what they really mean, no matter how they deliver the message.

When you are not clicking with a client, recognize it and adjust your strategies. Maybe you're coming on too strong, or maybe you're not coming on strong enough. Always have a sense of what your clients think about you.

QUESTIONS FOR YOU

- *Are you aware of how clients perceive you?*
- *What present lifetime relationship opportunities are you missing out on because you are not properly reading people?*

10. Adjust Your Strategies As Needed

One of the most enjoyable aspects of business for me is discerning how people want to be treated and adjusting strategies to meet client needs. That's why reading clients is so important.

Determine exactly how clients like to be treated, and treat them that way.

When you build relationships well, you become an excellent detective, learning the particular likes and dislikes of each client. You adjust your strategies based on how clients want to be treated, and in the process you start building lifetime relationships.

Excellent businesspeople are like chameleons with their clients; they adjust to clients. If their clients are chatty, they are chatty. If their clients are businesslike, they are businesslike. You determine how your clients behave, then act accordingly. I'm not suggesting that you become phony or insincere. I am saying to be shrewd, empathize with your clients, read them well and follow their lead.

QUESTIONS FOR YOU

- *Are you reading clients well?*
- *Are you adjusting your communication style to build better rapport?*

11. Always Do What You Say You Will Do

Good rapport is based on trust. Another strategy to build trust is to always do what you say you will do. Most businesspeople set themselves up to lose by overpromising and underdelivering. They have their initial meeting and promise to have a proposal or additional information in the next couple of days, then they get tied up with something else and miss the deadline. The next time they talk to the client, they can't understand why the client is upset.

Ask clients when they need your product or service, and then deliver it early.

I used to get caught in the same trap. I made promises I couldn't keep. Finally, I got smart and started asking clients, "When do you need it?" Nine times out of ten they would give a date later than I expected.

Even though I had tried for more leeway on the delivery date, I always sought to deliver the project to clients before the date they stated. Be sure to understand clients' expectations, make promises on the basis of those expectations, and then consistently live up to your promises.

QUESTIONS FOR YOU

- *Have you ever delivered more than you promised?*
- *How did you feel afterward?*
- *What did your clients say?*

12. Implement Your Clients' Suggestions

Imagine saying to your clients: "I took your advice." "I did as you suggested." "I followed your suggestion."

If your clients are like mine, they love to give advice and direction. I found I developed greater client rapport when I tried clients' suggestions and thanked them for their advice when the suggestions worked. When clients recommended I research the competition, or call a certain person, or read a book, or check out a Web site, I did just what my clients recommended. I found my clients were surprised that:

- **I had listened and actually heard what they were saying.**
- **I actually followed their suggestion.**
- **I thanked them for their advice.**

Besides building rapport, I usually learned something new and valuable in the process.

When a client next suggests you do something, try following her advice. What do you have to lose?

Make sure your words and actions always agree.

QUESTIONS FOR YOU

- *Are you acting on clients' suggestions?*
- *Are you thanking them for their advice?*

13. Use Humor to Disarm Your Clients

When appropriate, use humor. At times, businesspeople have their defenses up. A great strategy to break through these defenses is to make your clients laugh. One of the safest ways to do that is to make light of yourself. Besides adding laughter to the dialogue, you show clients that you don't take yourself too seriously.

Use humor judiciously and at the proper time. When a client is extremely upset, it's not the time to make a joke. Be sure that your client understands that although you have a good sense of humor, you take his or her concerns very seriously and you're no fool. You don't want to be considered a clown or to be accused of making light of what the client takes seriously. Also, never joke about anything that is remotely controversial.

TRUE STORY: Now I Always Check My Zipper Before I Speak

I once presented a workshop to 50 managers from Cellular One in Pennsylvania. The day I spoke to these managers had been a particularly busy time for me. I had eight speaking engagements in three states over a three-day period.

I had driven up to Bethlehem, Pa., to speak on leadership. I had only 45 minutes with the group before I had to return to Maryland to address 75 bank managers about lifetime clients.

Offer clients assistance even if you will not be immediately rewarded.

Before I spoke to Cellular One, I had to use the rest room. I was so focused on my talk and how much leadership material I could squeeze into 45 minutes that I neglected to zip my fly. I proceeded to get up in front of the 50 managers, men and women, and start to speak. I noticed the crowd was more interested in my talk than usual, and everyone wore a big smile. At the break, my contact informed me that my fly was halfway down. My face turned as red as the tie I had on. After the break, we all shared a good laugh. Needless to say, I now always check my zipper before I get up in front of an audience.

The moral of the story: I now have a great opening story for future audiences.

QUESTIONS FOR YOU

- *Are you disarming clients with humor?*
- *Do you make light of your own mistakes?*

14. Make Yourself Useful

Another strategy for building lifetime rapport with clients is to be a positive influence and to offer your assistance whenever you can. This assistance might be as simple as opening a door for a client, offering to make a telephone call or picking something up for them. It might be going the extra mile and properly addressing a client's concern by picking up on the client's concern and walking it through your organization to resolution, instead of letting it drop. It might be setting your client up with another service that can meet its most pressing need, before it can use your service. It might be making dinner reservations, procuring tickets or arranging a golf outing.

Always be a pleasure to do business with.

Whatever the situation, offer assistance. Make yourself useful. This is an excellent way to show your clients that you care about them and not just about the profits their business will bring you. In the long run, anything you can do to help clients will help you. This is a partnership, and you need to look out for your partner's interests as well as your own. Take these client rapport-building strategies and use them to forge stronger relationships with your clients.

QUESTIONS FOR YOU

- *On a scale of 1 to 10, how effective are you at building lifetime client rapport?*
- *What steps will you take today to improve your rapport-building skills?*

(continued)

THINGS TO DO "MONDAY MORNING"

- **Always look for the best in your clients.** Give them the benefit of the doubt.
- **When you have an opportunity to meet face-to-face with a client,** take it.
- **Find common ground with your clients.**
- **Never eat a meal alone.** Invite a client or vendor with you.
- **Speak your clients' language,** using terminology and concepts you both understand.

Hear What Your Clients Are Actually Saying

LIFETIME TOOL

6

CUSTOMER ONCE, CLIENT FOREVER

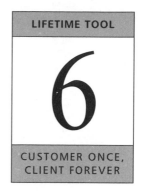

In this chapter, I'll share:

- **Twelve strategies to help you listen more effectively to clients**

Listening is one of the most important and most underutilized business skills. Just as the ability to listen is critical to success in your personal relationships, so too is it critical to success in business. When you want to build lifetime relationships with clients, you must hear what clients are trying to convey.

Most clients don't know exactly what they want. You need to take the time to help them determine their exact needs. Once you do this, you will inevitably make the sale and begin a lifetime relationship.

Many salespeople have difficulty listening to clients. We all know the stereotype of the smooth, fast-talking salesman who won't let the client get a word in edgewise. Those who fit the stereotype think the key to making a sale is to talk the client into it, without giving him a chance to express his concerns. They begin "selling" before they've heard what the client's needs are. They drone on and on while the client gets more and more upset. Not surprisingly, these businesspeople don't realize what's happening—they're too busy talking. Such salespeople never realize that listening is the key to success—hearing the client's needs and concerns, and thus being able to respond effectively. Excellent, successful salespeople are those who are outstanding listeners. Not only do they make the initial sale, they also build the foundation for a continuing relationship.

I once accompanied a salesperson to his prospective client's home, where the client spent the first five minutes describing how his dog, a German shepherd, had been terrified by the previous night's storm and had hidden under a table. When we left 45 minutes later, the same salesperson noticed a jar of dog biscuits and commented, "Those are pretty big dog biscuits; do you have a dog?" I can only imagine what the client thought.

The most successful businesspeople listen first.

It's not only salespeople who have tin ears. Most businesspeople don't take the time to properly listen to those around them and to their clients. My experience with all types of organizations (with sales from $1 million to $1 billion) has shown that often it's the managers and owners who do not listen. So much valuable information could be learned in business if people would just listen to each other.

In all my years of consulting, I have found the best listeners in organizations are usually the customer service representatives—the people who are on the front lines talking to clients daily. Perhaps it's because they're in constant contact with clients, so they can't help but sharpen their listening skills. Whenever I work with an organization, I'm always eager to spend time with these front-line people. They invariably have the most accurate view of what is going on in a company because they listen to what's going on around them.

Seven hundred years ago, St. Francis of Assisi suggested in a prayer, "Grant that we may not so much seek to . . . be understood as to understand." This ought to be the mantra for everyone in business—whether you answer the telephone, generate the sales, provide technical support, sign the paychecks or lead the troops. Take time to understand people. And to understand people, you must listen!

TRUE STORY: Careful Listening Saved Me a Trip to the Hospital

A couple of years ago, my friend Jennifer asked me to meet a friend of hers, Tom, who had just received his MBA. She told me Tom was in his mid forties and very bright. Jennifer thought Tom and I could work together, or at least partner on some projects. I am always open to new opportunities, so I called him and we set a time to meet.

When you listen well, you will clearly hear your clients' needs.

Jennifer was exactly right. Tom was very bright and energetic. As he spoke, I knew he was a great teacher. He had a wonderful ability to use diagrams to illustrate his points. He had so much energy. However, as we talked, I began to learn, piece by piece, something even more important about Tom that would seriously affect any relationship we might have had.

He told me that as an intern during his first year of business school, he had had a difficult time getting the owner of a deck company to understand and accept his research on the buying trends of clients. He told me that at their second meeting, they almost "came to fisticuffs" over his findings on buying trends. I began to feel a little uneasy. What kind of consultant are you if you have to resort to violence to get your point across?

Ten minutes later, Tom mentioned that he and a friend of his, a lawyer, were suing someone together. Tom also told me they had successfully sued someone else in the past. We had just met, and 20 minutes into the conversation about the possibility of working together, I learned he had almost come to blows with a client and he had a propensity to sue people.

By listening carefully, I deduced that if he did not come to blows with a client, he might come to blows with me if we disagreed on a plan of action. (I was more concerned about his attacking a client.) I also deduced that if I escaped bodily injury, I would probably be sued.

Listen carefully to what clients are trying to convey to you.

I did not want to be attacked, and I certainly did not want to be sued. So, when we finished our conversation, I thanked Tom for his time, and in an effort to stay clear of hospitals and lawyers' offices, I decided not to pursue a business relationship with him.

The moral of this story is that through active listening, I saved myself a lot of potential headaches—and perhaps kept my nose from getting broken. While Tom had many characteristics I would want in a business associate, his propensity for antagonistic relationships ultimately made him unsuitable. No matter how bright he was, or how much energy he had, it was not worth running the risk of being attacked or sued.

Active listening means:

- **Paying attention**
- **Asking pointed and direct questions**
- **Restating the message to make sure you understand what the speaker is saying**
- **Looking and listening for the emotions behind the words.**

Active Listening Strategies

Lots of business books talk about how important it is to listen better; few offer concrete suggestions. From many years of workshops,

I've put together some strategies participants have suggested to sharpen listening skills. Here are strategies you can use to listen more effectively to your clients.

1. Stop Talking

I start with the most basic strategy and the one I hear the most from workshop participants. This means just what it says. Do not talk—listen. Focus all your attention on the person speaking.

Seek first to understand, then to be understood.

Notice what percentage of the time clients talk compared with the percentage you talk. If you are selling, an 80/20 split (the client talks 80 percent of the time and you talk 20 percent of the time) is appropriate for your first client appointment. If you are in customer service, the split is probably 85/15. What is most important is to let clients speak first and to hear them out.

TRUE STORY: Speaking Your Client's Language

When I first started selling, I called on a client to whom I had submitted a $100,000 proposal. The buyer told me he had "pretty much awarded" the contract to another firm. I consulted with a senior salesperson in my firm, and he suggested we go visit the buyer together. I called the buyer and he agreed to meet with us.

I was young and inexperienced and thought I was all ready for our appointment. I was ready to talk product, delivery and pricing. The senior salesperson told me to sit tight and follow his lead.

We met with the buyer, and it turned out he was a big football fan. He had gone to the University of Arkansas and had been friends with the coaching staff and some of the players. My associate saw his interest in football and got him talking about Arkansas football. He talked, we listened.

We spent an hour and a half in this man's office, and all we talked about was Arkansas football. We talked about past and present seasons; we talked about players and coaches. The buyer told a hilarious story of how years ago the star running back had robbed a local convenience store wearing his game jersey, with his name emblazoned across the back. But I was getting more and more frustrated because we were not talking about products and services.

Listen 80%, talk 20%.

At the end of the meeting, the buyer told me to put the submittals together and send them to him and he "would see what I can do about the contract." A week or so later, the contract came in the mail.

I learned two very simple but powerful lessons:

Stop talking and listen to your clients. While I was itching to sell the client with facts and figures and control the conversation, what I really needed to do was find some common ground to establish a relationship. The senior salesperson had a lot more experience than I did. He knew that, first, the client had agreed to see us, which was a victory in itself; and that, second, the client was comfortable enough to talk with us for a long time about a mutual interest, football.

Never ever give up on any project. When the client said he had virtually awarded these contracts, I could have dismissed the project as hopeless, or a trip to his office as a waste of time. If I had dismissed the project, I would have missed out on a $100,000 opportunity and the opportunity to develop an ongoing relationship.

When you want to improve any relationship in your life, stop talking and start listening.

QUESTIONS FOR YOU

- *How often do you let clients speak first?*
- *Who does most of the talking: you or your clients?*

Listen generously to your clients.

2. Give Your Clients Your Undivided Attention, and Listen Generously

While your client is speaking, forget any pitch or response you may have. Don't be thinking, "I can't wait till my client stops talking so I can tell him about this."

Listen! Clear your mind and make a genuine effort to hear what your client is trying to convey to you. Sometimes the greatest gift you give anyone is simply to listen.

If you listen carefully, you'll know what to say when your client finishes. Sometimes you need time to think over what clients have said. Clients are likely to be impressed that you're seriously considering what they've said instead of just delivering a stock comeback.

In addition, don't carry your prejudices and biases into the conversation. Keep an open mind and be prepared to change your own opinions if your client has offered compelling reasons why you should.

Don't think about all your events of the day, where your next appointment is, what your last client said to you, what you may have planned that evening. Put yourself in this client's shoes and listen to what she is trying to say to you.

Listen generously by giving clients your undivided attention—no ringing telephone, no interruptions, no reading your pager, no accepting other telephone calls, no putting a client on hold to answer another call. Turn off your cell phone. Put your pager on vibrate and wait until after your meeting to read it.

Don't carry your biases and prejudices into client conversations.

Your conversation should not be about convincing your client of your way of thinking. It should be about one human being truly listening to the needs and concerns of another human being. That is the proper way to build a lifetime business relationship.

QUESTIONS FOR YOU

- *Are you giving your clients enough time to express themselves?*
- *Are you giving your clients your undivided attention and prohibiting any interruptions?*
- *Are you keeping an open mind about what your clients are saying?*

3. Notice Your Client's Tone of Voice and Body Language

Ninety-three percent of communication is nonverbal. Sometimes clients' tone of voice or body language will convey more than their words.

Pay attention to your client's voice tone; it will tell you quite a lot. Is she happy, sad, angry, peevish, noncommittal or upset? For example, if your client sounds harried when you call, you might be better off acknowledging how busy he or she seems and asking for a better time to talk.

In face-to-face meetings, what is the client's body language telling you? People communicate not only with words; they also send messages with their bodies. When you next meet with a client, notice the following:

- **Are his arms folded across his chest?**
- **Is he looking out the window or otherwise failing to meet your eye?**
- **Is he tapping his fingers on the desk or constantly looking at his watch?**

Read your clients' body language.

If a client is doing any of the above, you may suggest that this appears not to be a good time and ask if you can reschedule the meeting. You may also want to ask if everything is all right.

Conversely:

- **Is the client's body posture open and receptive to your message?**
- **Is he smiling?**
- **Does he stand and smile to greet you? Does he clasp your shoulder?**
- **Is he leaning toward you?**
- **Is he maintaining eye contact with you?**
- **Is he "hanging on your every word"?**
- **Does he appear relaxed?**

If your clients do any of the above, this is a positive sign that they are open to you. If they are not receptive to you, reread and practice if necessary the strategies discussed in the previous chapter on building rapport (Lifetime Tool 5).

QUESTIONS FOR YOU

- *Are you listening to your clients' voice tone?*
- *Are you reading your clients' body language?*

4. Take Detailed Notes

This is my favorite strategy for improving listening, and one of the most effective. Taking notes helps me immensely in business. Not only can you refer to your notes if you forget some details of a conversation, you can also improve your memory through the act of writing.

Many years ago, during my first sales meeting, I didn't take notes. I just smiled politely and sat quietly as my client revealed all I needed to know to make the sale. Unfortunately, since I hadn't taken any notes, all that valuable information—what the client was looking for, his previous experiences, what was most important to him—was lost. It all went in one ear and out the other. I neither remembered what he'd said nor was able to refer to notes to refresh my memory.

Take notes using your clients' exact words and phrases.

In making notes, write down clients' exact words on important points—especially when they are expressing their needs. When you explain to clients how your product or service will help them, isn't it much more effective to repeat back to your clients their exact words and phrases? "Mr. Client, you mentioned that 'price is a driving concern.' This product will meet your needs at the proper price." People are best persuaded by their own words.

You have lots of options for where to put your notes. Many computer-contact management programs (such as ACT, Maximizer and Goldmine) have fields for you to insert notes. I suggest taking notes on a copy of your client proposal because you'll have all the important information you need in one place when you need to refer to it.

Wherever you take notes, make sure it is a place that is easily accessible. I have found it helpful to note both the date and time I spoke with a client. Not only will this help refresh your memory of the conversation but it also will help you impress your client with your precision. Should any dispute arise, having this information will strengthen your position.

Here's a quick example of the kind of notes that you could take:

> **9/25 10:25 AM**—Called Dale Bruss, not in, left message.
>
> **9/28 2:30 PM**—Reached Dale, received our proposal, not ready to do anything yet, call mid Oct., said price was a "little high" and delivery was "CRITICAL." Call her in 2 weeks.
>
> **10/9 9 AM**—Called Dale and set up meeting for 10/20 to discuss proposal. She asked me to "take a second look at our price" and reinforced the importance of delivery.

Taking detailed notes improves your memory and provides a paper trail.

In addition, guess how your clients will feel when you pull out a notepad and begin to take notes. How would you feel? Notice their expression and posture when you do this. They know that you're seriously interested in what they have to say. Of course, asking permission to take notes is always a good idea. Rarely have I had a client say no.

If you are selling, taking accurate notes is a win-win situation. You win by learning a lot about your potential clients. You immediately gain credibility and respect in their eyes because you have taken the time and effort to take notes. Your clients win because you will effectively serve them by understanding their needs. Will your competition take the time to do this?

In taking notes, not only do you increase the chances of a sale, you also gain valuable information that you can refer to months or years later. I have closed sales from notes I had from a meeting two years before.

You also have accurate information to share with your sales managers, customer service staff and others in your company. With this information, they can help you develop the strategies for creating a lifetime client.

5. Repeat What You Think You've Heard

People are best persuaded by their own words.

When you practice all the strategies described above, you should be able to repeat to your clients their needs in their exact words and phrases. This is absolutely critical to successful listening. You need to hear someone well enough to say back to them, "If I heard you correctly, you would like me to . . ." or "Did I understand correctly when you said you wanted . . ."

If you have not heard a client correctly, he or she will tell you so. This is how you develop a greater and deeper understanding of clients' needs. When you start using phrases like this, you are well on your way to listening more effectively and building lifetime relationships.

6. Ask Insightful Questions to Understand Your Clients' Needs

Part of good listening is asking good, probing questions. If you are in sales or customer service, remember that your time with clients is an opportunity to interview them, to get a better understanding of their exact needs. Your questions should come from not only your knowledge of your product and service but also the information you get from listening to the client.

By listening closely to what a client says, you can pose questions that will give you a deeper understanding of his or her needs. At the same time, you demonstrate to the client that you have been listening carefully.

You want to gather as much information as you possibly can on clients' needs. I discuss in depth what questions to ask in the next chapter. Right now, though, let me share a story that demonstrates the importance of asking good questions.

Ask clarifying questions: "If I heard you correctly, you said . . . "

TRUE STORY: How Three Simple Questions Improved Performance

One of my clients is an estate-planning firm that prepares living trusts. The firm holds open seminars. After the seminar, the firm offers attendees a free hour of consultation with an attorney.

I was able to take the firm's least productive lawyer and make him the most profitable (not the top salesperson, but the most profitable) by changing the questions he asked clients. Working together, we developed three simple questions for him to ask at the outset of each client consultation. He asked the three following questions and listened carefully as clients responded:

What prompted you to attend our living-trust seminar? This question usually uncovered people's true motivations. By his client's answer, the lawyer could tell who was sincere about completing estate planning and who was just looking for another way to pass a morning. (Yes, some people have nothing better to do with their time but go to a free seminar.)

What did you think of our seminar? If the firm's client praised it, the lawyer was probably close to a sale. If the client didn't, the lawyer had a pretty good idea of how much "selling" he needed to do. Again, he could judge the sincerity of clients by their responses.

What are your goals in estate planning—that is, what do you hope to achieve? The answer to this question helped define what is really important to clients.

Good listening prompts better client questions.

If clients expressed a concern about taxes and probate at the outset of a meeting, throughout the meeting the lawyer pointed out their tax and probate exposure. Again, this question helped sniff out any pretenders.

Because we had the lawyer ask all three questions at the outset of the meeting, within the first five to ten minutes he had a pretty good idea of how serious clients were.

QUESTION FOR YOU

- *Are you asking clients insightful questions like the ones above?*

If you are in sales, you want to enter your next client meeting prepared with specific questions tailored to that client. One of the best questions to ask all clients is, "What are your exact needs?"

Remember, most of your clients don't know exactly what they want or need or what you have to offer. You need to assist them. The better you can help clients clarify their needs, the better you serve them, and the easier making the sale and building the lifetime relationship becomes.

You need to determine what is most important to clients. Is it price, delivery, service, or quality of product? What really matters to them? Most clients have not answered this question because no one has asked them.

For example, if you are a financial adviser, is your client most concerned about:

- **Making the most money possible?**
- **Having peace of mind with investments?**
- **Successfully transferring assets from one generation to another?**

Asking probing, insightful questions also shows your clients that you're seriously interested in understanding their needs. You are making the effort. You want to understand their needs.

Always ask clients, "What exactly are your needs?"

7. Maintain Eye Contact

Maintaining eye contact is an excellent way not only to show respect but also to keep your attention focused on clients. If you're not looking directly at your clients, you're missing an excellent opportunity to absorb as much information as you possibly can.

In addition, remember the eyes are the "windows to the soul." One of the best ways to evaluate clients' intentions is to look directly into their eyes. For example, if clients say they are going to give you the business and while they are saying this they look away, you may not get the business. It's a lot harder to mislead someone when you are looking into his or her eyes.

QUESTION FOR YOU

- *Are you consistently maintaining eye contact with your clients?*

8. Maintain an Open Body Posture and Keep an Appropriate Distance

Along with maintaining eye contact, you should

always maintain an open body posture when listening. Part of listening well is having a relaxed and open posture. Be aware of the message your body language may be sending a client. If you have your arms folded across your chest in a defensive posture, do you think you are truly hearing what a client is trying to convey to you? Will your client feel comfortable with you and have confidence in you?

Maintain eye contact: Clients' eyes are the "windows to their souls."

Maintain an appropriate distance from your client. If you're too close, you could be invading that person's personal space, which he or she may see as threatening or at least uncomfortable. However, don't be too far from the client. You want the client to feel you are having a friendly, relaxed conversation and that both of you can easily hear and speak to each other. With this in mind, when you're not in your own office, it's always a good idea to ask the client where you should sit.

If a client comes to your office, don't sit at your desk, which suggests you are in a more powerful position than the client. Pick a more equal arrangement—at a separate table or in two comfortable chairs away from your desk, or in a conference room. Sit beside a client in more of a partnership posture rather than across the table, in what may be considered an adversarial position.

If you are in customer service, have an open body posture when you are speaking on the telephone. It's just as effective to have open body posture over the telephone as it is in person.

9. Let Your Clients Know You Are Listening

Let clients know that you are listening to them by nodding at the appropriate times or saying something such as, "Yes, I understand."

Don't do this as a conditioned response to feign interest while you're actually thinking about how you're going to make the sale. Do this because you are truly listening. Let clients know you are in the conversation with them. This is especially important over the telephone when clients cannot tell whether you are paying attention to them.

When you have an opportunity to meet face to face with a client, take it.

10. Notice What Clients Do Not Say

When you're building a lifetime business relationship, it's important to notice not only what clients say but also what they don't say. In selling, for example, it's important to note what clients aren't telling you. When you begin to listen carefully, you hear what clients are *not* saying.

For example, you will notice some clients focusing exclusively on service, yet rarely talking about price. Service is critical to them. Conversely, other clients will focus on price and not talk about service. This is a good time to introduce and reinforce the importance of service.

11. Listen for the Feelings Behind the Words

The old adage of life is also true in business: "It's not what people say, it's why they say it." Listen carefully for the feelings behind the words that prompt clients to say what they're saying.

When you want to understand clients better, look carefully for the possible feelings behind the words. For instance, say you are a financial broker and you meet a potential new client. In your meeting, the client vents his feelings that he thinks financial advisers are useless. You could become defensive and fire back to defend brokers. Or, with intelligent questions, you could probe this feeling. Chances are the client has had a bad experience with a broker and is a little gun-shy.

The key here is not to take the clients' words at face value but to figure out what has prompted clients to say what they are saying.

It's not what clients say, it's why they say it that matters. Listen for the meaning behind their words.

12. Actions Always Speak Louder Than Words

While listening carefully is critical to forming a lasting relationship with your clients, actions always speak louder than words. You will understand clients more completely by not only listening more carefully to what they are saying, but also reading their actions. Let me share an example.

TRUE STORY: The Hat Exchange

I had a client whom I literally had to call 30 times to get an appointment. I was so elated to be there that as soon as I walked in, as a good-will gesture, I gave him some of our company baseball hats. No sooner were the hats out of my hands than he gave me the same number of his company's hats. How should I have read that?

When I have asked people in workshops what this meant, they've usually said it was a good sign. He was being generous. However, in view of the fact that I had made 30 calls to get this appointment, I read his action as meaning he didn't want to be indebted to me. He didn't want to feel obligated. I give him three of my hats, he gave me three of his hats. We were even. He didn't owe me anything.

It turned out my company did not get the project I was meeting with him about. However, I continued to persist, and we eventually won business from him.

Conflicting messages. If a client says you are going to get the business you're seeking, yet he does not return your telephone calls, you are probably not going to get the business. In such a situation, you might casually drop in to say hello. Try to figure out what the stumbling block is by asking more questions about clients' needs, whether those needs are currently being met and, if so, by whom?

Hear what your clients are *not* saying.

QUESTION FOR YOU

- *Are you properly reading clients' actions?*

A Last Word on Listening

Listening is hard work but incredibly rewarding when you do it properly. It is an active, not passive, process; you exert energy when you listen. When scheduling your appointments, remember and call up the energy necessary for proper, active listening.

Listening is such an important skill in business that you should reread this chapter every couple of months. When you want to further your business career, improve your listening skills. Attend any seminar or workshop that can improve your listening skills. You can never do enough to sharpen them.

(continued)

THINGS TO DO "MONDAY MORNING"

- **Listen 80% of the time, talk 20%.**
- **Read your clients' tone of voice and body language**—people use more than words to communicate their true thoughts and feelings.
- **Take detailed notes,** using your clients' exact words and phrases.
- **Ask insightful questions** to gain a deeper understanding of clients' needs.
- **Listen for the feelings and emotions** behind clients' words.

Asking the Right Questions

LIFETIME TOOL

7

CUSTOMER ONCE, CLIENT FOREVER

In this chapter, I'll share:

- **Questions to ask your clients so you can better serve them and develop lifetime relationships**
- **The importance of precise communication**
- **The benefits of asking the right questions**

To exceed clients' expectations, we need to completely understand their needs. To understand needs, we must ask the right questions. No matter where you work in an organization, you will better serve your clients and find greater fulfillment in your work by asking better questions. Just as businesspeople can always improve their listening skills (Lifetime Tool 6), they can also always improve their questioning skills. Most businesspeople squander their precious time with clients by not asking the right questions. The following story demonstrates the importance of asking direct questions.

TRUE STORY: Warren Buffett Asks the Right Questions and Saves GEICO

Warren Buffett is a true legend in business. Few individuals have enjoyed the long-term success on Wall Street that he has. Buffett is especially known for his ability to rescue either financially distressed companies or companies fending off attempted hostile takeovers. (In the reading list at the end of this book is a wonderful biography of Buffett, thoroughly researched and well written by Roger Lowenstein.)

One of Buffett's greatest success stories is GEICO, an insurance company headquartered in

Washington, D.C. During the early 1980s, GEICO's stock plummeted. The company was on the verge of bankruptcy before Buffett bought any stock. In fact, the situation was so dire that in Lowenstein's exact words, GEICO, "once a seemingly invincible company, was on the brink of becoming the biggest failed insurer ever."

Most people looked at GEICO and saw disaster. Not Warren Buffett—he saw opportunity. He requested a meeting with James Byrne, who was GEICO's CEO at the time.

Always seek to gain a more complete understanding of your clients' needs.

Buffett and Byrne met late one evening at the home of Katharine Graham, the publisher of *The Washington Post,* in Georgetown. Buffett handled the meeting like a textbook business appointment. He spent the majority of his time listening. When he did speak, he asked very pointed and direct questions.

Most American CEOs would have spent the entire time telling Byrne what to do (probably knowing very little about the actual situation) or, worse yet, droning on about their past successes: "I did this, I did that."

Buffett did the exact opposite. He "interviewed" Byrne into the wee hours of morning. Buffett saw his meeting with Byrne as an opportunity to learn as much as he could about GEICO. Byrne was impressed with the insight of Buffett's questions and commented later, "I'm sure I did 80 percent of the talking"—the figure I suggested, in the last chapter, for the client's portion of a conversation.

Buffett, for his part, was so impressed with Byrne's answers that he purchased a significant portion of GEICO stock at a low price and ultimately made a tremendous profit. Not only did Buffett make a killing on GEICO stock but, in the process, he increased the overall value of the company overall and saved it.

This story demonstrates the power of asking good questions. Buffett could have spent their valuable time together telling Byrne of his own past successes. Instead, he demonstrated his genius by asking insightful and direct questions and learning all he could about the opportunity in front of him. With the information he gained by asking pointed and direct questions, he maximized his investment and rescued a company destined for bankruptcy.

Ask better questions to gain a greater understanding of clients' true needs.

QUESTIONS FOR YOU

- *Are you asking your clients the right questions?*
- *Do you approach your business calls with the same laserlike precision as Buffett's?*

Questions to Ask to Develop Lifetime Clients

Of the dozens of questions you could ask your clients, the following are most effective in developing lifetime relationships. Take note: At the root of all these suggestions are five key questions: Who? What? When? Where? and How much?

"What Exactly Are Your Needs?"

This question (a refinement of "How can we help you?") is far and away one of the most important (and least asked) by businesspeople. How can you serve clients effectively if you don't know exactly what they need?

Whether you are selling automobiles, homes,

computer software, financial services, consulting, or anything else, you need to know exactly what clients' needs are. The better you know and understand these needs, the better you can fulfill them and the sooner you'll develop a lifetime relationship.

Develop and write down questions before you meet with your clients.

We've said most clients don't know exactly what they want. They have a vague idea, but they need knowledgeable businesspeople to help them understand their precise needs. For instance, a client may sense that he needs help with financial planning, but he doesn't know exactly what steps he should take and in what order to take them.

This is where true relationship-building occurs. You demonstrate to your clients that you do care about their concerns. By finding out exactly what your clients' needs are, you begin to build bonds that last a lifetime and that encourage your clients to refer others to you.

To elicit your client's response to "what exactly are your needs?" good questions include:

- **What are your goals?**
- **What do you want to achieve from our work together?**
- **What is your desired result?**

If you're in sales, you should ask these questions the first time you meet with prospective clients. Their answers will tell you a lot about how serious they are. If your clients give you pretty detailed answers, they've done their homework. If they don't give you detailed answers, they either are not as ready as they appear to be or they may not have enough trust in you. Knowing that will help you determine how to proceed.

The nice thing about asking this partnership-type question—"What exactly are your needs?"—

is that it beautifully opens the door to three excellent follow-up questions:

1. **What work like this have you done in the past?**
2. **Whom did you use?**
3. **Were you happy with your experience?**

When you start with these questions, ten minutes into your client meeting you will have gained a wealth of information. In addition, your clients will start to see that you have their best interests at heart. You begin to establish yourself as the trusted adviser. In essence, you position yourself almost as a doctor who wants to relieve a client's pain. Remember my one client who asks, "Where's the pain?"

Ask clients what their experience has been with your product or service.

TRUE STORY: How Two Questions Completely Changed a Sales Call

I once went on a series of sales calls with a young man who had just started in business. He was selling sophisticated, high-pressure valves and fittings. On our first call together, he met with an engineer who showed him a detailed drawing of a new type of system the engineer was building. The salesperson automatically assumed the engineer needed one or two high-pressure valves. The young salesman asked a couple of minor questions about how much pressure each valve had to handle. It turned out to be a standard call that led to a small order for two valves—maybe some repeat business, maybe not.

A couple of hours later, the young salesman was in another engineer's office with a similar call. Frustrated that his first call of the day had not gone as well as he would have liked, the salesman altered his strategy. His first questions were different: "What are you trying to accomplish? What do you want this system to do?"

These two questions totally changed the call. This appointment could not have been more different from the first one. The second engineer opened up and explained the entire process of his system—sharing a wealth of knowledge. While the engineer was speaking, he began to smile and became enthusiastic about his experiment. In learning more about the client's system and the client's goals for the system, the salesman was able to better advise the client and offer more and better equipment to contribute to a more successful experiment. In addition to laying the groundwork for a lifetime relationship, this salesperson learned just how drastically two simple questions could change an ordinary sales call.

Ask clients to rank the priority of their needs: What's most important to them?

Two similar calls produced two different reactions—all because of two simple questions.

QUESTIONS FOR YOU

- *When was the last time you asked a client, "What exactly are you trying to achieve?"*
- *Are you gaining a complete understanding of your clients' needs?*

"When Exactly Do You Need the Product or Service?"

One of the great challenges is serving a client in a timely fashion—that is, not on your time clock but on your client's clock. To best serve a client, you need to know exactly when he or she needs your product or service.

If you're in customer service, you no doubt have clients who rant on and on about a minor issue. Asking them this question brings them back to the matter at hand. If clients are not sure when they are going to proceed or purchase, this approach gets them thinking about a date. If they tell you, "Sometime in the future," press for a more accurate date: "When exactly?"

Remember your goal is to serve clients—to be the trusted adviser—and understanding clients' schedules is a large part of doing that.

Be sure to remind your clients of allocation of work, factory schedules, weather difficulties, the implications and costs of procrastination, and whatever else is pertinent to your delivering your service or product. Always leave a meeting with some idea of the delivery schedule, and make sure your clients understand the cost of their inaction.

An initial client question should always be: "What's your budget?"

QUESTION FOR YOU

- *How effective are you at determining when clients need your product or service?*

"What Is Your Budget or Price Range?"

You should ask this question early on. If a client's budget is ridiculously low, you need to know that immediately and advise the client. By doing this, you display your expertise and help clients understand what they can realistically expect. As a trusted adviser, you need to let clients know whether their expectations and budget are in agreement.

Here you also have an opportunity to feel clients out. How committed are they? If clients rattle off some pretty tight figures, you know they are prepared and are probably shopping around. If a client's response is wishy-washy, maybe he or she is not as committed as you think or doesn't trust you enough yet.

"Who Decides on the Purchase and When?"

You must know, and the earlier the better, who the ultimate buyer or decision maker is in your client's company. It does you no good to put on a stellar presentation in front of a person who cannot make the decision about buying.

Always speak to the decision maker.

In my early years of business, I lost business and the opportunity for lifetime relationships by talking to the wrong people—those who were not the ultimate decision makers. My sales and my self-confidence increased when I started to ask who was buying and then asked to speak directly to that person.

TRUE STORY: Missed Opportunities, or Who's Really Buying?

In my early years of selling, one of my clients had at least 25 project managers. I would bid a project to a project manager and assume that since I gave the price to that person, he or she would award the project. This was not so. After some missed opportunities, I learned that one man, to whom I had never spoken, was the decision maker. I would never win a bid to this company unless I spoke with him.

I could spend $1,000 bidding on a project. I could then wine and dine those project managers, take them to lunch, give them sports tickets (which get more expensive by the day), and treat them to a round of golf (also expensive). All this would be in vain, because the bottom line was that only one man awarded projects. And I was not speaking to him!

I became more successful when I started asking clients, "Who will ultimately buy?" Once I found out who the ultimate decision maker was, I directed my efforts toward him or her.

QUESTION FOR YOU

- *Are you putting yourself in front of the decision makers?*

"On What Criterion Will You Ultimately Base Your Decision?"

Determine what's ultimately important to your clients.

This is one of my favorite questions. Whether you are in sales, customer service or management, you need to know what is most important to clients. How will they decide how to proceed after they have received a slew of proposals? What is most important to your clients—price? quality? service? experience? Does your client have a brother-in-law in the business who will get the business no matter what you do?

What is important to you may not be important to your client. You need to find out what *is* important to the client. Asking your clients to tell you their most important criterion is fair. After all, you are taking your time and energy to work with them.

If the criterion is price alone, all your subsequent efforts should be directed to working the numbers tightly and going in with your most cost-effective proposal. Then move on and find another client to bid where price is not the single most important issue.

I find that businesspeople who complain about losing clients haven't done a good job of asking these questions at the beginning of their client meetings. If they lose a client, it's not the client's fault; it is the businessperson's fault for not clearly understanding the client's desires.

When I ask clients what is important to them,

I'm surprised at how few mention price as their number-one concern. To most clients, price is not the key concern. Sometimes it's quality, sometimes service, sometimes value, sometimes delivery. It all varies depending on the client.

When you find out the criterion, you can tailor your proposal and strategy to meet your clients' exact requirements. When clients tell you service is important to them, make sure they completely understand how well you will serve them. It is a good idea to include any letters that you have received from previous clients that stress your outstanding service.

Be sure to ask new clients how they learned of you.

QUESTION FOR YOU

- *Are you asking clients what's most important to them?*

"How Did You Happen to Call Us? Who Referred You?"

When you receive a request out of the blue from a new client, it helps to know how that person got your name and telephone number. It might be from an association you belong to or an ad you placed. It might be from a business or personal referral. The client may have just looked in the phone book for someone offering your products or services.

After I began asking this question, I found I had many calls on small projects that happened to be referred by my best clients. While I always endeavored to treat all orders equally, it helps to know who was referred by what clients, so you can thank the person giving the referral and also learn more about what the new client expects.

When I processed those small orders quickly

and kept clients happy, I found that many large transactions would follow. It didn't take me long to realize that clients were sending up trial balloons—testing our service with small orders to see how we would do.

QUESTION FOR YOU

- *Are you politely asking clients how they happened to get your name and number?*

If you want a lifetime client relationship, ask what it will take to gain one.

"Any Special Conditions or Concerns I Should Know About?"

To best serve client needs, you must turn over all rocks. You will be surprised how much valuable information you can find out by asking this simple question. I often learned how important delivery or coordination with other firms can be.

If you're a financial adviser, you might learn a particularly valuable and sensitive piece of information regarding a client's financial past or future by asking this question. In addition, by asking this question you demonstrate to a client how thorough you are.

"Who Else Is Competing for Your Business?"

Again, you are taking your time and energy to work on a project. Don't you want to know who your competition is? Why not ask? If you do so in a professional and respectful manner, you may be surprised how much prospective clients will tell you.

Remember, how your clients answer this question will tell you a great deal about how much rapport you have developed with them. If they dodge the question, you'll know you have not gained their trust and still have work to do.

When I asked clients this question, I was surprised at how many told me exactly who their other contacts were. Maybe five percent would not say. That was all right, too, because it told me that I needed to build more rapport with the client.

Always ask clients who else they are working with.

What was really interesting was that about one-third of my clients told me my company was the only one they were getting a price from. In this case, they sometimes asked if I had any suggestions on other firms they should contact. Obviously, this is an enviable position to be in.

QUESTION FOR YOU

- *When was the last time you asked prospective clients who else they were speaking to?*

"Who Have You Used in the Past?" "What Was Your Experience?" "Were You Happy With the Results?"

In Lifetime Tools 2 and 3, we talked about being a client's trusted adviser. Once you have done the legwork, you get to reap the benefits. Since you have positioned yourself as the trusted adviser, you can ask these questions and get more background information on your clients. Wouldn't it help to know who your clients have used in the past and what they thought of these competitors? Why not ask?

The obvious follow-up question is: "Were you happy with the service?" You will either learn valuable information or your clients will try to elude you. Either way you win. If they try to elude you, you know you don't have a proper level of trust. If they tell you the truth, you learn how to better serve them through knowing what they liked or didn't like about the previous service.

"What Can We Do to Earn More of Your Business?"

You always want to get a sense of how much business you're doing with a client. Why pursue new clients if you have not maximized all the business you can with existing clients?

Make sure all your clients are aware of all your services.

As a good businessperson, you should always be aware of what percentage of its business a client is doing with your firm. Rarely is it 100 percent. To achieve all of a client's business, you have to work for it. The first step in this process is to determine how much of the client's business you do and ask exactly what you need to do to attract more business.

"Are You Aware of All Our Services?"

Are all your clients aware of all your services? When I was in the construction business, I was surprised how few of my clients replied "yes," when I asked this question. In fact, if I asked ten people, I might have gotten one confident "yes."

Make all your clients aware of all your services. You accomplish this by asking this question and reminding clients often of all the services your firm provides.

Including a brochure that lists all your products and services in mailings to your clients is another good idea. Update your Web site to include all your services. One of my clients increased his sales by simply listing all of his services on his stationery.

"How Can We Develop a Lifetime Relationship With You?"

If you want a lifetime relationship, why not ask directly what it will take to develop one? In all my years in business, I had only one client tell me that we would not have a lifetime relationship. He told me he would never give all his business to one source. Ultimately, I respected his decision and still had the opportunity to do 60 to 70 percent of his work.

Be respectful when asking clients questions.

If I asked ten clients for their lifetime business, I eventually won eight of them as lifetime clients.

QUESTION FOR YOU

- *When was the last time you asked a client, "What can we do to earn all your business?"*

"What Holds You Back?"

Again, as the trusted adviser, your concern is seeing that your clients' best interests are served. If you completely believe in your business, you should be able to ask clients what keeps them from using your service. They will either have legitimate reasons that make sense or have smoke screens. After you spend time listening and asking questions, you deserve to know exactly what clients are thinking.

Ask the Right Way

You don't want to bombard your clients with these questions. You don't want to ask in a threatening and interrogating manner. You want these questions to be part of an easygoing, give-and-take conversation. These are also questions you ask after you've given clients the proper time to express their needs themselves.

Practice all the listening strategies that we shared in the previous chapter. In addition, you may want to write down your questions before a client appointment. Keep them by your telephone to ask your next prospective client. Research clients and the type of business they're in, so your questions will be intelligent and produce useful answers. Your client will be impressed by your diligence and knowledge.

QUESTION FOR YOU

- *Are you maximizing your time in front of a client by asking targeted and direct questions?*

The Benefits of Asking the Right Questions

By asking the questions I've just discussed, you will set yourself and your clients up for an invaluable payoff that will bear long-term dividends:

You will gain valuable information. When you get answers to all the preceding questions, not only do you have excellent information to properly serve a client but also you begin to develop a relationship. If after gathering all this useful data you still have problems, take all you've learned to your manager or someone you respect, and work together to arrive at a winning strategy.

Remember an important point: Clients are more likely to give you information at the outset of a project than at any other time. If you wait, for

TRUE STORY: PRECISION AVOIDS CONFUSION

I always remind people in workshops to practice precise communication. Consider this example of a not-so-precise message.

Someone from the firm that cleans my office called and left a message asking if the firm could switch its cleaning day "from Wednesday to Friday." Does this mean clean on Friday only for this week or switch to Fridays permanently?

You might think that because the person who called did not say permanently, it would be just a one-time thing. It turned out to be the opposite, which was not clearly explained in the voice-mail message.

This vendor's poorly worded message caused confusion and extra work for itself and for me.

Practice precise communication.

example, until the delicate negotiation stage to ask what other firms your client is talking to, chances are your clients will not tell you. Trust me, I found out the hard way. Ask up front!

You will show clients that you are on the ball. Are your competitors asking these types of questions? Probably not. When you ask these questions, you will appear sharper and wiser than your competition. Clients will take you more seriously because they see that you take them seriously. In addition, you clearly demonstrate that you are interested in exceeding their expectations and earning their long-term business.

You will help set the clients' agendas. If your clients did not have a game plan or overall strategy before they met with you, you have just helped them develop one. Ninety-five percent of businesspeople miss the boat here. This is where the real selling and relationship-building takes place—in helping clients understand their needs. If you help clients set their buying strategy, do you think you will have a better chance of winning the sale and the lifetime relationship? Absolutely!

Selling and building lifetime relationships is a process, and a large part of the process is helping your clients discover exactly what they need. A challenge in business is getting clients to be specific. You can help them by asking targeted and direct questions: "How much exactly would you like to see sales increase?" and "Where exactly do you feel your sales force is coming up short?"

Always seek more specific data from your clients.

Help clients be precise. As their trusted adviser, you can't serve them unless you know exactly what is going on. In asking specific questions, you also help them clarify their needs for themselves.

THINGS TO DO "MONDAY MORNING"

- **Listen first,** then ask precise questions to gain a more complete understanding of clients' needs.
- **Ask clients on what criteria they will ultimately decide how to proceed:** price, service, experience or another concern.
- **Ask clients what their previous experience has been with your product or service,** and listen carefully and respectfully to their responses.
- **Prepare for your next client meeting** by writing down exactly what questions you will ask the client.

Systemizing Your Business

LIFETIME TOOL

8

CUSTOMER ONCE, CLIENT FOREVER

In this chapter, I'll share:

- **What a business system is**
- **The key steps in systemizing your business**
- **Key principles to process business**
- **How to maximize profits**

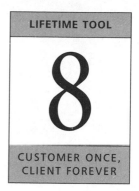

Everyone wants the sale; few want to deal with processing the actual order. That's ironic, because the critical order-fulfillment stage is where you'll find the *real* opportunity to earn lifetime clients and greater profits. Most businesses are so concerned with short-term profit that they neglect it. When you properly process an order, you accomplish two worthwhile objectives: You solidify a lifetime relationship with your client, and you maximize your profit. In this chapter, I'll offer specific strategies to continually improve order processing.

What Is a "System"?

Webster's dictionary defines the word "system" as follows: "A group of interrelated elements forming a collective entity; a network; a set of interrelated procedures; the state or condition of harmonious, orderly interaction." A system simply means that every step, from the initial client sales call to the sending of the final invoice, is clearly charted for everyone—you, your client and your associates—to recognize and follow. Think of it as an internal conveyor belt that allows you to process a client transaction properly and efficiently, whether that transaction has five or 500 steps.

A system means your lead becomes a quotation, then a sale, then a production order, then a billing, then a collection, and finally an opportunity for a lifetime client. All the steps of your business flow together naturally.

Perhaps a good example of a business system is what Henry Ford accomplished with the assembly line. Before the assembly line, cars were built with parts from all around Detroit. Ford did something radical yet simple: He brought all the departments together, under one roof. Everything that was needed to produce Ford cars was in a single location and part of a single system—one that revolutionized manufacturing.

The real opportunity in business is in successfully fulfilling an order and completing the transaction.

If you are an architect or engineer, your sketch becomes a blueprint that in turn becomes a real physical structure. Every piece works together. In your business system, too, every piece must have a reason for being and will affect the rest of the system. The sooner you see this, the easier it is to continually improve your system and earn lifetime clients and greater profitability.

QUESTIONS FOR YOU

- *Does this definition of a system accurately describe your current business operations?*
- *What is your system for processing business?*
- *Are all the steps of your business system clearly delineated for everyone to see and follow?*

Why You Need a Business System

The sale and the lifetime relationship begin with the order. Everything beforehand is just talk; what matters are the actions you take to fulfill clients' needs. You must have an established system in place to process the order.

Most lifetime clients are either won or lost in this process. When you improve your system, you greatly improve the likelihood of developing and maintaining lifetime client relationships. When things go wrong, I find most companies blame their people. It's not their people, but their lack of a business system.

Lifetime clients expect excellent service after the sale.

Businesses have two major functions—sales and fulfillment (delivering the product or service). Wherever you work in a company, it is very important to make sure that you contribute to exceeding clients' expectations. If you are in customer service, order fulfillment or technical support, you are critical to this process. One of the most important people in the business process is the first person who answers the telephone. Is it answered politely by the second ring? Is the client greeted with a friendly voice? Is the client's call routed quickly to the proper person?

Receptionists, customer service reps and technical support people are the unsung heroes of an organization. Whether a client stays for life depends not on all the promises salespeople make but on how well these unsung heroes serve the client during order fulfillment.

As you continually improve your system and become more efficient, you continually improve your client relationships. When you accomplish these three things, you automatically increase your profitability. It's just that simple.

The Benefits of a Business System

It's not enough just to develop a system—you and everyone else in your company need to use it, constantly critique it and continually improve it. When you create and fine-tune your system, you will be able to do the following:

Properly serve the client. My primary reason for creating a system for the first company I worked for was to serve my clients as efficiently as possible.

At that point in my career, I was still learning about the value of lifetime clients, but I did sense how important it was to win client loyalty. It didn't take me long to see that when I created a system and took care of clients, they would come back again and again and tell others about our service. This repeat and referral business made my job and life easier and made me more profitable.

How your receptionist answers the telephone signals how clients will be treated.

Process transactions to generate billings, so you can get paid. As I became more seasoned, I recognized the importance of monthly billings and collections. The sooner my company could serve a client, the sooner we could bill him and receive his payment.

Sales are only an *opportunity* to make a profit. In essence, through sales, clients are allowing you an opportunity to serve them and generate profits. *Nothing happens until you serve the client.* You can have $20 million in sales on the books, and that's exactly where it will stay—on the books. You need to convert those sales to billings as soon as possible.

Earn the maximum profit possible. Since you're already doing the work, why not make the maximum profit that you can? The more you improve and refine your system, the sooner you can effectively serve the client, the sooner you will be paid, and the greater profitability you will enjoy.

Gain valuable marketing opportunities. When you create a system that enables you to serve your clients effectively, you also create excellent marketing opportunities. Your greatest opportunity to earn new business is through your existing clients. If you are in customer service or in order fulfillment, you probably don't recognize all your potential marketing power. Clients will tell other people how you have treated them—how well you manage your business. This is invaluable advertising.

You can take out a $100,000 back-page ad in the *Wall Street Journal* touting your firm or take that same $100,000 and invest it in improving your system so your clients will spread the word about your excellent service. Which do you think will provide a greater return over the years?

Process every client transaction as if it is your last opportunity to serve your client.

Set yourself apart from the competition. When we "sell," all we use are words. What ultimately matters is action—the service you provide. Anyone can promise anything. The question is, can you deliver? Improving your system is an excellent way to distinguish your firm from the competition.

Make your job easier and less stressful. I actually backed into creating and using a system. One of my motivations was to make my job easier and less stressful. As I mentioned earlier, I was getting 20 to 30 calls a morning, 95 percent of them asking where I was and why I was late. I was getting called on the weekends and, most important, my clients' concerns were coming home with me. I had to figure out a way to reduce all the incoming calls.

Unconsciously, I ended up creating a system to process the work. If you find your job overly challenging and stressful, you need to either create a system or fine-tune the one you have.

TRUE STORY: How Using a Business System Helped Me Earn a Lifetime Client

The more systematic your business becomes, the more profitable it will become.

When I was selling in the construction industry, I was trying to close two good-sized contracts with a large international firm. Not only had we done little business with the company, but we had never worked with this project manager it assigned to these projects. In short, this was a challenging sale.

Over a 12-month period, I repeatedly called the project manager, Craig, without much luck. We had a couple of brief and insubstantial telephone conversations. I suggested that we meet, which we finally did—briefly. He was noncommittal about doing business with us.

For the next six months, I continued to call without reaching Craig and without getting any return calls from him. By this time, I figured both projects were gone.

One day, out of the blue, Craig called me and said he was ready to do something. He wanted to give one contract to me and the other contract to our competition. He asked me how I felt about that. Obviously, I said I wanted both projects but would appreciate any business we were awarded.

We accepted the one order and did all the things we would normally do (that is, followed our established system): made an architectural submittal for approval, followed up on it, scheduled field measurement, ordered material, scheduled installation and closed out the project. Nothing fancy or out of the ordinary was involved; it was just a run-of-the-mill project. Throughout the project, I made sure the client didn't have to track us down; we initiated all the calls to report on progress and made sure all was going well. If the client ever did call us, we immediately returned the call.

Six months later Craig had another project for which I submitted a proposal. Before I ever had a chance to call him to follow up (and remember all the times I had to call him before) he called me and said the following: "The job is yours, at the price you bid. Last time I gave one job to you and one to your competition. I never heard any complaints about your work and service, but I did have a nightmare of a time with your competition. I never want to hear that name again, much less do business with that company."

Efficient business systems guarantee lifetime clients.

The moral of this story? My system not only made my job easier but won me repeat business.

Five Steps to Systemizing Your Business

You can begin today to take five key steps toward an effective system that will improve your performance and increase your profitability:

1. **Recognize and acknowledge that you need a system to process business**
2. **Organize your system to achieve the best possible performance**
3. **Establish operating procedures and guidelines**
4. **Analyze the output of your system**
5. **Continually improve the system.**

I want to underscore that no matter where you work in an organization, you can apply these strategies. If you can't implement a system for your entire organization, you can at least implement a system for yourself.

Step 1. Recognize and Acknowledge That You Need a System

You need a system to properly process your business. Some misguided companies expect a smile to be their entire customer service program. It's not enough. To be successful, you must have underlying systems that reinforce your business efforts.

Flow-chart each step of your business system.

I suggest you begin to look today at your entire operation—from your first client contact to the final bill on a project and the retention of the client—as an interrelated system.

Get your team together with every phase of your business represented and sit down and write out all the steps involved in properly serving a client. This listing should include every step from the client's first telephone call to final billing and all client retention strategies. Just completing the above exercise should refine the process. For greater success, create a flow chart to help everyone visualize the process, especially the relationships between tasks.

Recognize that all the steps work together. Every part of your process builds on itself.

TRUE STORY: From Chaos to Order to Profits, Part I

One of my clients offers an excellent example of a system. Three years ago, this company wrote its orders six different times. In a nutshell, this was the "routine":

A prospective client called, and the salesperson who took the call wrote down the customer's initial request on a piece of paper. Quotations were complex because the company sold numerous products, with many long part numbers. It was not uncommon for quotations to have ten to 20 line items with these long part numbers.

The salesperson next rewrote the request on the quotation form and faxed it to the client. At this point, the order had been written twice.

Clients who wanted to place an order frequently added or deleted products from the quotation form. When the client gave a go-ahead, the salesperson wrote the order a third time and turned it over to customer service.

Make sure every step in your system has a purpose.

Customer service reviewed the order to make sure everything checked out and rewrote the order for purchasing—the fourth time the order was written. (Are you getting tired yet?)

Purchasing wrote the purchase orders for each vendor—number five.

Accounting wrote the order again for billing purposes—the sixth (and final) time.

This is a rather large company that processes a couple of hundred orders a month, so you can imagine the lost time in duplication of work.

Two issues are present here: duplication of effort and increased possibility for error. How many staff hours were spent essentially writing an order six times? How much money did this cost the company? In Lifetime Tool 1, Continually Improving Yourself, we shared the importance of measuring your performance. Measuring the effort exerted by this company to process its orders would produce some daunting figures—surely significant enough to show that developing a better system would be a good investment.

The second issue in this example is the higher possibility for error that is created by rewriting orders so many times. With all this rewriting, coupled with the long and involved part numbers, the possibility of someone making an error skyrockets.

It's the quality of transactions, not the quantity, that ultimately matters.

QUESTIONS FOR YOU

- *Are you duplicating your efforts?*
- *Can you measure the duplicated efforts?*
- *How many times are you writing an order or transaction?*

TRUE STORY: From Chaos to Order to Profits, Part II

This story comes to a happy conclusion because my client did develop a system to convert chaos and inefficiency to order and efficiency by customizing its computer software to create a smooth and seamless order-entry system.

Here's what happens now:

When a client calls with a quotation, the salesperson opens a customized computer order-entry screen and enters all the necessary information into the fields displayed. This form becomes the source document for all future work related to that order.

When the client wants to amend an order, all the salesperson—or anyone else, for that matter—has to do is pull up the screen and make the necessary changes with a few keystrokes.

The sales department can electronically send the order to customer service, which quickly reviews and electronically forwards it to purchasing.

Notice the information is entered only once and then sent electronically to the necessary departments. All the rewriting of the order is eliminated.

By fine-tuning its system, the company achieved the following benefits:

Decreased costs. The company increased its profitability because it eliminated the staff hours, and resulting costs, of writing orders six times.

Increased speed. Rather than passing cumbersome folders from department to department, staff members now send all information electronically with a few keystrokes.

Improved efficiency. Rather than being written six times, the order is written once. Instead of rewriting orders, employees can devote their efforts to more pressing issues. This client later created the position of "expediter," whose sole responsibility is to call vendors and expedite orders.

Increased sales. Company sales rose fourfold, to close to $100 million. Part of this incredible increase was due to the company's implementation of this seamless order-entry system.

Improved morale. In place of a cumbersome system, the company had a streamlined process. The company set its staff up to win by bringing the best technology to its office. Rather than having its people trudging orders and thick folders from department to department and getting frustrated by having to duplicate work, the company handled all aspects of processing an order electronically.

The single most important and efficient way to motivate, reward and inspire your people is to roll up your sleeves and create the most efficient system possible. In the reading list at the end of the book I have included some books about how to energize and motivate your associates.

The more efficient your system, the more profitable you will be.

Motivation is not about cookies and trips and prizes. It's not about "employee of the month." It's not about fluffy motivational speakers. It's about creating the most efficient organization and system you can. To build the most efficient system, you need your people's input and support. Do you want 99 quarters of uninterrupted growth? Remember Sam Walton's visiting his stores to ask managers what was not working, and chiding them for failing to deliver bad news?

People want to work in a company that has taken the time and energy to lay out precisely how it tracks its business and its clients.

QUESTIONS FOR YOU

- *Are you setting your people up to win?*
- *When was the last time you asked someone how you can improve?*

Step 2. Organize Your System to Achieve the Best Performance

After you recognize that you have a system and have made a flow chart of all the steps involved in the process, you must organize your system for the best possible performance. Your goal should be to produce your product or service in the fewest possible steps, without sacrificing quality.

You must make sure that you eliminate duplication of effort and that every step in your system has a specific purpose.

Creating the most efficient system is much like evolution—every step has a specific meaning or use. If it does not, it is useless and needs to be eliminated. To be successful and best serve your clients, you should completely computerize the process just as my client did in the preceding stories. I have worked with many companies that have partly computerized their process, but a truly efficient system must be completely computerized.

Once you develop a system, everyone must follow it.

Total computerization of your system offers two advantages:

It enables you to carry out all the steps quickly and efficiently. The system not only rids your process of redundancy and inconsistency in data collection, but also it enables you to see, with a simple keystroke, where any order or transaction is at any given time. The computer prompts the next step in the process. The computer, in effect, becomes a "conveyor belt."

It enables you to create an outstanding reservoir of data that can be analyzed to help you become even more efficient. This is an important opportunity to analyze valuable data that will help you better serve clients and become more profitable. I discuss this further in Step 4.

Step 3. Establish Operating Procedures and Guidelines

We have a system. We have organized the system for the best possible performance. Now we need to focus on the people in the process.

You need to create a set of business operating

procedures or guidelines for all your associates to follow. This simply means that every single step in order processing is accounted for—down to who calls the client and when—and that everyone involved is aware of his or her role in the process.

Create a flow chart showing exactly how you deliver a product or service, and share this with your associates. Everyone in your organization needs to understand this process thoroughly enough to be able to explain it to a client. If your process is too difficult to explain, that's a clue that you need to continue refining it.

Provide a one-page contact list that tells clients who does what at your company and how to reach them.

In addition—and this is equally critical—your clients need to be educated on the process. Too few companies take the time to properly educate their clients on how their transactions are processed. Clients need to know exactly what to expect—who gets involved, when, and why. In client relations, the old adage is absolutely true: "The best surprise is no surprise."

For example, if you run a financial-services company and are handling sensitive, and somewhat confidential material, you need to advise your client on who in your office will see this material. As a client, there is nothing worse than having someone you do not know, or have not been told about, call you and begin discussing personal and sensitive information.

QUESTIONS FOR YOU

- *Do your clients know exactly how their business will be processed and what is expected of them?*
- *Do all your associates know exactly what is expected of them?*

Step 4. Analyze the Output of Your System

If your business is systemized, it will produce data to be analyzed. Most businesses miss an outstanding opportunity to track and analyze these facts, and thereby serve their clients more efficiently.

How much more profitable will you become when you are able to track, analyze and share the following information?

- **How many orders or transactions your company processes a month**
- **The percentage of orders or transactions that are on time, ahead of schedule and late**
- **The average processing time of an order or transaction**
- **The level of client satisfaction.**

Determine the capacity of your business system.

Once you've collected this information, the form in which you share it with your people is important. I have seen presidents and managers of organizations walk out to the plant floor, and show their people pages and pages of wide, green computer sheets with rows and rows of numbers, and expect instant understanding.

Conversely, I have seen managers convert that same data into simple colored bar and pie charts and share them with their people with much greater success. Greater success means your people can see more clearly the results of their work and are motivated to contribute even more. You must track the information properly and share it effectively.

Most companies spend a great deal of time measuring sales. Companies that direct the same attention to measuring their orders find even greater success.

QUESTION FOR YOU

- *Are you able now, with a single keystroke, to determine the status of all your open orders and transactions?*

> **"Theories come and go, but fundamental data always remains the same."**
> —MARY LEAKEY, ARCHEOLOGIST

Can you have too much business? Absolutely! That's why it's imperative that you constantly measure and analyze the output of your system. Until you measure your output, you have no way of knowing what your system's capacity is.

I recently called my mortgage company and was on hold for more than ten minutes. When I commented on the inordinate hold time, the manager told me that they were swamped with client calls and that my ten-minute hold time was standard. In fact, she even said that if you called the competition, you'd find the same hold time. (Do you wonder why I suggested in the first chapter competing against yourself and not others?) Perhaps the mortgage company should develop a better model that gives it a clearer idea of the optimum business it can handle so it can properly serve its clients without ten minutes on hold.

Why "box scores"? When you track the output of your system, you become able to deliver weekly or monthly box scores to their associates. To help your people be successful, show them exactly how they are doing.

For instance, a company should show its salespeople the following figures on a weekly basis:

- **Business bid**
- **Transactions closed**
- **Transactions or orders in-house**
- **Profitability on orders in-house**

After all, knowing which products and services

are profitable and which are not allows a salesperson to better serve a client.

You need not be in sales to use box scores successfully. For instance, in customer service, you can deliver the following box scores to your people:

- **Number of client transactions processed**
- **Number completed on time, ahead of schedule, and later**
- **Number and nature of client complaints**
- **Percentage of client complaints resolved**
- **Overall client-satisfaction index.**

Seek to deliver your product or service in the fewest possible days, without sacrificing quality.

The bottom line: The more specific information you can show your people, the greater the chance they will improve their performance.

A quick word on the client-satisfaction index: Just as I showed you in Lifetime Tool 1 how measuring the quality of my workshops dramatically improved performance, assigning a one-to-ten rating to your client interactions can help you improve, too.

I'll offer more specific client feedback strategies in the next chapter.

Monitor your turnaround times—your clients do!—and continually seek to improve them. Never miss deadlines, and always look for ways to beat them. If it usually takes you 30 days to deliver your product or service, find a way to do it in 15 days.

Process transactions and orders as quickly as possible. Every day you delay processing an order, you lose money and the potential for a lifetime client. As motivation for processing an order, every day an order sits, staple a $5, $50, or $100 bill to it, depending on the size of the order. You might as well. That's the cost of not moving it through the process.

Time is money!

QUESTIONS FOR YOU

- *Are you sharing the right information in the proper format with associates?*
- *How much more successful will you be when you use box scores?*
- *Are you processing transactions as soon as you can?*
- *If you aren't, what's holding you up?*
- *What steps will you take to improve?*

Always look for ways to improve your business system.

Step 5. Continually Improve Your System

No matter how good your system is, it can always be improved. The best resources to help you improve are your clients and your associates. I discuss in greater detail in the next chapter how to best gain valuable client feedback.

Two immediate suggestions to gain feedback are to ask both your people doing the actual work and your clients this critical question: "How, specifically, can we improve our service to you?"

To be precise, you constantly want to ask yourself and your people the following questions:

- **Are all your clients receiving the same level of service?**
- **Are you delivering the same level of quality on each order or transaction?**
- **Does this level of service merit repeat and referral business?**
- **Are you converting these referrals into sales and, ultimately, into lifetime clients?**

If you are overwhelmed with client orders, or feel you are not operating at peak capacity, use these five steps to systemize your business.

Here are key principles for processing your

business more effectively and profitably.

Take responsibility. Be accountable. The single greatest action I took in order fulfillment was to take complete responsibility for serving the client. I assumed responsibility for all the steps and actions that existed between me and my client after the sale. I did not wait for the client to call me or to push his or her own transactions through our organization with repeated telephone calls; I called the client.

As I've said before, live by the credo that clients should call you only once and that thereafter you should proactively call them and request the information necessary to process their orders in a timely fashion.

I found that the more responsibility I took, the easier and less stressful my job became, and the more my business increased. Plus, clients were friendlier and easier to deal with when I was initiating all the telephone calls.

No matter where you work in an organization, decide that it is your complete responsibility to see a client transaction through and to exceed the client's expectations.

After a sale, personally assume responsibility for all the interactions between you and your clients.

QUESTIONS FOR YOU

- *Are you taking complete responsibility for each order?*
- *Are you actively calling clients to complete their transactions?*
- *What pushes transactions through your organization: your clients' repeated calls, your initiative or your system?*

Raise your personal standards. Next, you must hold yourself to a higher standard, to ask and expect more of yourself.

I found great success when I beat delivery deadlines. If delivering an order normally took four weeks, I told the client to expect it in four weeks, but I worked toward completing it in two weeks. If it took four weeks, I was all right. I had that two-week cushion. If I completed it in two weeks, I was Superman in the eyes of my client.

Continually educate your clients on how your business operates.

Holding yourself to a higher standard also means returning all client calls the same day. You have heard the expression, "Underpromise and overdeliver." Let that be your motto.

Federal Express revolutionized the overnight delivery business by promising a 10:30 A.M. delivery time—and then meeting it.

QUESTIONS FOR YOU

- *What you are doing today to underpromise and overdeliver for your clients?*
- *What can you do to revolutionize your industry?*

Don't tolerate mistakes. In addition to continually improving performance, become less tolerant of mistakes. Track mistakes, get to the root causes of them, and eliminate them.

For instance, if you are in customer service, begin to track client complaints by category: poor service, faulty products, poor delivery or company error. The more specific you can be, the easier it will be to spot and correct trends. Aspire to deliver the highest level of client service that you can.

QUESTION FOR YOU

- *Are you tracking mistakes and seeking to eliminate them?*

Make sure your clients and associates understand the system. As I said earlier, make sure your clients clearly understand what exactly will take place after the sale. What exactly will your firm do? Who will contact them? When?

Few companies realize this is where true "selling" occurs, so most miss a valuable opportunity. They rarely take the time to educate clients on how their orders will be handled. Chances are, if you can't clearly explain to clients what will happen, you don't have a good system in place and will not be able to exceed clients' expectations.

Proactively call clients after the sale to update them on project status.

Put everything in writing and transmit it to your clients by fax or e-mail as soon as possible. Make sure that your clients clearly understand all the details.

If any misunderstandings or disagreements occur, they need to be resolved at this stage. This preventive medicine will greatly increase your chances of developing lifetime clients. If you do not clearly communicate with clients, you increase your chances of a future dispute.

In the end, you will always lose a dispute by losing the client and ultimately the lifetime relationship. To make sure your system runs smoothly and that everyone is informed of problems that may cause delays, make sure your associates understand how the system works and their roles in it. Impress on them the importance of keeping the lines of communication with clients open.

Standardize your process. Your order process should be so finely honed that each order or transaction follows the same steps. The more you standardize your process, the better, because you achieve consistency in delivering your orders.

One of the best examples of standardization is

McDonald's. When you order a hamburger (whether you are in the U.S., France or China) that hamburger goes through all the same production steps. You receive the same product wherever you are.

QUESTIONS FOR YOU

- *Is your process completely standardized?*
- *Is your operation as finely tuned as possible?*
- *What steps will you take today to standardize your order process?*

Call clients after you have completed transactions, to measure their satisfaction and confirm they will return.

Maintain a dialogue with clients. Just as in the sales phase, continue to maintain a dialogue with your clients during the order process. This continued dialogue is crucial to creating the accountability you need to process a client transaction in the fewest possible days and to the utmost client satisfaction. This dialogue also helps cement the lifetime bond with your client.

I have learned that staying in touch with a client is more important after the sale than before. Here is your opportunity to deliver on all the promises you made during the sales process. This is where you will build lifetime rapport. Clients expect you to call them persistently when you are trying to get their business; they don't expect you to call with the same persistence to fulfill their orders. Do this and you will keep clients for life.

Specifically, let me offer what I think is an excellent strategy for maintaining the dialogue with clients after the sale. If you receive many orders or service requests from clients, perhaps you can customize your computer software so you can send a client an e-mail message that lets the client know the following:

- **When you received the order or service request**
- **The order number it got when it was entered into your system**
- **When the order will be delivered**
- **A customer service contact name, and telephone number or e-mail address.**

You do have the option of sending a postcard with the same information; however, I think it's critical to computerize your process.

Encourage clients to e-mail requests to you.

In addition, let clients know immediately of any snafu. I had more than my fair share of delays with orders. Afraid to anger a client, I wouldn't tell him immediately that an order would be delivered late. I found that because of this, clients were upset with me for two reasons—for the delay, which was usually outside my control, and for not being told immediately about the delay. The latter I could and did correct.

When I wised up, I advised clients of delays immediately. Once I started doing this I not only felt better, I rarely had clients get angry about a delay. Instead, they usually thanked me for keeping them in the loop.

You also don't want to be the last one to know about delays, so you need to ensure that your company's internal communication lines are open and functioning. Make sure your people understand how important it is to communicate with others in the process about any problems or potential delays.

You can choose many methods for communicating information about your business system. I'm surprised at how few companies take full advantage of newsletters, e-mail, Web sites and other media besides telephone calls to communicate with their clients.

I recently worked with a client who had just

started to receive work orders by e-mail. I was in the manager's office, and he had a stack of old-time pink telephone message sheets with work requests scribbled on them, and one e-mail work request with all the information neatly printed out. Which do you think was easier to process? All the client needed to do with an e-mail work order was click and send it to the proper department. If a client e-mails you a request, all the information you need is already written. If your system is set up properly, you can simply forward the request to the correct department.

Track running times of transactions from date initiated to time completed.

I also recommend that, if you are not already doing so, you call after an order is delivered to ensure that the client is happy. This follow-up telephone call is critical to securing a lifetime relationship. Whatever a client is not satisfied with, take care of immediately.

Don't lose the clients you've worked so hard to gain through a lack of communication or a miscommunication!

QUESTIONS FOR YOU

- *How well are you communicating with your clients after the order?*
- *Are you letting clients know about delays as soon as you can?*
- *Is your company properly using all the media available to communicate internally and externally?*
- *Are you calling clients with the same persistence after the initial sale as you did before the sale?*

Process transactions immediately. Don't procrastinate with transactions. Nike says it best: "Just do it!"

Usually our greatest challenges are not what we think they are. We sometimes become so consumed with the competition and things out of our control that we neglect the issues that are in our control. In business, I've found that procrastination, not competition, can be the greatest hindrance.

Time is money. Processing an order quickly gives you two benefits:

- **The sooner clients are served,** the happier they are, the sooner they will return, and the sooner they will tell others about you, which increases your business.
- **The sooner clients are served,** the sooner they will pay your bill.

Respond to all clients' inquiries the same day, if not sooner.

QUESTION FOR YOU

- *Do you have any orders or other transactions sitting on your desk right now?*

Promise clients later delivery; deliver sooner. We do well in "selling" when we underpromise and overdeliver. When applicable in order processing, promise later delivery and deliver sooner.

I have seen businesspeople lose a relationship by making promises they can't deliver. I think they get so overwhelmed by all they have to do that they are always thinking they have to play catch-up.

In my earlier days, I was stretched thin. I was trying to do too much. I always felt behind. Because I felt behind, I made promises I couldn't keep. I finally wised up and started to ask clients, "When do you need this?" Invariably clients gave me later deadlines than I had anticipated. Don't promise what you can't deliver.

If clients don't like the longer lead time for delivery, you find out immediately and can adjust delivery to satisfy them.

Know exactly what you earn; that's the figure that ultimately matters.

Work backward to see if you can complete tasks in parallel. Once you've laid out all the steps for your system, work backward in your system to see if you can complete tasks even if they are not in the "normal" order. See if doing some tasks in parallel can speed things up. Boeing offers an excellent example of this:

Years ago, *Fortune Magazine* reported that Boeing used to take up to 18 months to build an airplane because it built its planes sequentially—first it built the fuselage, then the right wing, then the left wing, and finally the tail section. To speed up production time, Boeing began building its planes in parallel, making the individual sections at the same time and then assembling them, almost like a kit. Production time was cut in half.

Personally, I have found it helpful whenever I ordered material or started a service to submit the invoice immediately to accounting. The invoice then returned to my desk within one or two days, ready to send to the client when the project was complete. It was then up to me to process the remaining business as quickly as I could so I could send out the invoice. When I prepared invoices in this manner, three significant events occurred:

- **Having refined my system,** I was now more motivated than ever to order material and get an invoice to accounting. It was a good habit to form and practice.
- **No projects or invoices** slipped through the cracks. All the work I did was invoiced.
- **Because I gave the invoice to the accounting department,** I alerted others in the company to these projects. More hands involved made projects run smoother. That increased my motivation to push the project through as quickly as possible.

Measure client satisfaction and your profitability. It's not your perception of quality that matters, it's your client's perception. That in large part determines whether you will have a client for life. You need to measure this perception. The next chapter will offer suggestions on how to track client satisfaction.

Besides tracking client feedback, you need to track profitability. You can better serve clients and better run your business by understanding which products and services are most profitable.

Constantly compare estimated costs against actual costs.

What most improved the total quality of my efforts was tracking actual costs against expected costs. I developed a much greater awareness of money. If something was not done right the first time, my company would have to send someone out to take care of it, or I would go out myself. When I started to track the dollars spent on making these extra visits, we started to do work right the first time.

When I did well in sales, I enjoyed closing the sale. I spent all my time negotiating with clients. When I started to track expenses, I found that what I really enjoyed was the challenge of getting projects in under budget and in the fewest possible days without sacrificing quality. I started to spend much more of my time negotiating with our suppliers for the best possible price and the quickest delivery time for my client.

One of the best ways to improve your entire order-processing system is to track the overall time an order or transaction takes—from the date sold to the date completed. Once you start tracking the actual number of days involved, you begin to develop acceptable norms of delivery times. You want to improve the delivery times of the orders that fall outside the established norms.

Most businesses miss the opportunity to improve the inside of their operation. Use the strategies in this chapter to continually improve the internal operations of your organization. When you continually improve your service, you will attract lifetime clients.

Become your own client; experience your own service.

A client of mine found great success in tracking the complete running days—from order date to completion date—of his orders, excluding weekends. On his order-processing report, he listed in the far-right-hand column the running days of an order. He was able to quickly run through the report and, just by reading this column, get a good sense of which clients were being well served. If an order showed a figure of more than 30 days, he wanted to know why.

Ask for help. When necessary, reach out and ask for help. Ask your associates and your clients, and explore the wealth of resources available to guide and assist you in your pursuit of continual improvement. Pick one of the books from the list in the Appendix (pages 263-272), read it, and apply the strategies to your business.

QUESTION FOR YOU

- *Are you reaching out to the proper sources for assistance?*

(continued)

THINGS TO DO "MONDAY MORNING"

- **Develop appropriate business systems** to process business.
- **Customize your software** to better process your orders. Make sure all quotations can be entered into the computer and easily converted to an order-entry screen.
- **Analyze your order-processing data daily, weekly and monthly.** How many sales become orders? What is the average time spent processing each order or transaction?
- **Promise later, deliver sooner.**
- **Measure client satisfaction.**

Gaining Valuable Client Feedback

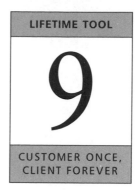

LIFETIME TOOL

9

CUSTOMER ONCE, CLIENT FOREVER

In this chapter, I'll share:

- **Why client feedback is critical in developing lifetime relationships**
- **How to set up a client panel**
- **How to design a useful client survey**
- **Other client feedback mechanisms**
- **What to do with the client feedback you receive**

I promised you at the outset of this book that *Customer Once, Client Forever* would offer a systematic and comprehensive approach to building lifetime relationships. If I didn't include a chapter on client feedback, I would be leaving out a crucial component in building lifetime client relationships.

While this chapter will offer a host of strategies to gain client feedback, please be aware that you need not have a client survey or a client panel to get feedback. Whatever your role is in an organization, getting client feedback is as simple as asking your clients, "How are we doing?" or "How can we improve?" You can pick up the telephone right now and call, or you can see clients in person. It doesn't matter how you ask for feedback; the point is that you do it.

Why Is Client Feedback Important?

The only way to truly understand clients' needs is to have an ongoing dialogue. You don't want to stop after you have delivered your product or completed the service. So much valuable information remains to be gained. You can't easily improve your service unless you know how your clients experienced your service.

Most companies do little in terms of client research. Fewer expend the effort to collect and analyze client surveys. Every time you don't gather client research, you miss a valuable opportunity to grow. Remember it's not your perception of your service that matters—it's your clients' perception.

If you are conducting business today and are not soliciting feedback or offering an outlet for your clients to voice their opinions, you are courting disaster. In the 21st century, you must allow your clients some sort of opportunity to critique your services.

To build lifetime relationships, get ongoing client feedback.

I am amazed by all the trucks on the road that solicit feedback on their drivers' skills: "How's my driving? Call 1-800 . . ." I wonder how many of these companies solicit similar feedback on their products and performance. How many ask the question, "How can we serve you better?" Further, I wonder how much more successful and profitable these companies will be when they implement client suggestions.

TRUE STORY: Why the Taurus Is Ford's Bestselling Automobile

The Ford Taurus is one of Ford's most successful automobiles—indeed, one of the best-selling vehicles in the U.S. Before the Taurus, Ford did very little client research on its new vehicles. Any research that was done was scant and was conducted after the vehicle rolled off the assembly line. That didn't offer much opportunity for continual improvement. This lack of research and assessment is all the more amazing when you consider what it costs to develop and produce a brand-new automobile: close to $1 billion.

However, when Ford developed the Taurus, it

did a great deal of research. Not only did it assemble many client focus groups to gauge potential clients' feelings about the vehicle, but it brought its divisions together to review and discuss the automobile. Obviously, its efforts paid off.

Moral of the story: When you want to develop a top-selling product or service, enlist the aid and support of your clients and associates.

Clients and associates often have valuable suggestions for improvement. Give them an opportunity to express them.

QUESTIONS FOR YOU

- *How do your clients rate your service?*
- *How do you track this?*
- *How much client feedback are you currently receiving?*
- *How much more profitable will you be when you receive client feedback?*
- *What products and services can you improve by asking for client input?*

TRUE STORY: Using a Client Panel to Get Feedback

A couple of years ago, an environmental engineering firm asked me to conduct a client panel so the firm could better understand how clients viewed their service. We invited six of its best clients. In front of the firm's entire office staff, we had a two-hour roundtable discussion that centered on two key questions:

- **What do you like about the firm?**
- **How can the firm improve its service?**

The panel was incredibly enlightening. In two hours, we learned a great deal about how to better serve clients. A vice-president of the company commented afterward that he learned more from those clients in two hours than he had learned in eight years working for the company.

Here are some key ideas and insights that we learned from the panelists:

They reinforced the importance of excellent customer service. For example, they wanted personal service from a human being. They all suggested installing voice mail but offering the option of going into someone's voice mail or speaking to a human being. The clients clearly told us they did not want to be sent directly into voice mail.

Clients expect to hear from you periodically.

They wanted to be continually educated on the environmental industry. In particular, clients asked to be updated on significant projects by receiving a one-page fact sheet, short and simple.

The panelists went so far as to request a "cheat sheet," a glossary of environmental terms, so it would be easier for them to understand the environmental business. In addition, they asked to be advised of new trends in the marketplace.

They wanted the firm to stay in touch with them. The panelists specifically requested that my client call every couple of weeks and say hello just to check in, even if they didn't have a project ongoing. "Remind us you are still out there. In the rush of other business, we sometimes forget about you," they told us.

Five of the six panelists commented that they valued the smallness of the firm, though the company was concerned about having only two offices—fewer than most of their national competitors. They preferred dealing with my client precisely because the company was small. Panelists said they liked dealing with people who could make quick decisions and institute action immediately, rather than being tied up in a bureaucracy.

The president of the firm had felt all along that the size of the firm was a drawback. He thought that because his company was not as large as its competitors, clients would not take it seriously. Through the client panel, he learned the exact opposite. His clients preferred the smallness of the firm. What the president thought was a liability was, in fact, an asset.

Give clients the option of speaking to a real person or going directly into your voice mail.

QUESTION FOR YOU

- *If you had a client panel, what would your clients say about your firm and your service?*

Suggestions for Setting Up a Client Panel

Below are some step-by-step suggestions for setting up a client panel. Treat your panelists well, and don't waste their time. The're doing you a favor and you may want their future business.

Preparing for the Panel

To have a successful panel, you must prepare for it. Not only do you want to conduct the panel smoothly so that your panelists feel comfortable, but also you want to ensure you'll get the best input from the panelists. Here are some suggestions for preparing for the panel:

Consider enlisting the aid of an outside facilitator

to help set up the panel and conduct it.

Invite a range of participants—those who have not used you before, marginal clients, happy clients, and perhaps one or two who are unhappy with your service.

Provide a meal—breakfast, lunch or dinner.

At every opportunity, ask clients, "How can we improve?"

Two weeks before the panel, ask all your associates who will attend the panel to draw up three to five questions they would like to ask clients. Have a meeting to review all questions.

One week before the panel, conduct a dry run. Set the room up exactly the way you plan to the day of the event. Have some of your people act as panelists. Fire off a couple of questions, making sure everyone is comfortable with the setting.

If you have not hired a facilitator, appoint one of your people to fill that role. This person should be skilled at eliciting more complete answers from client panelists.

At this mock panel, brief all your associates on all the panelists—what their history with your company has been and what their buying habits are. The better your people understand each panelist, the better the questions they can ask.

On the day of the panel, instruct all your people to act as hosts and to treat the panelists as guests. Your people should introduce themselves to panelists and make sure the panelists are comfortable and have everything they need.

Conducting the Panel

You want to conduct the panel smoothly and make the experience pleasant for your panelists. You also want to capture the valuable information shared. Here are some suggestions for conducting the panel:

Videotape and audiotape the panel. A recording documents the proceedings for easy review later.

Appoint one of your best listeners to take notes on exactly what the panelists say, in their precise words and phases.

Have a two-hour session with a short (five- to ten-minute) break after the first hour. Ask the panelists questions about your service: "What do you like about our firm? How can we serve you better?"

In their responses, encourage panelists to be specific: "Can you elaborate on that?" "How specifically can we improve that?"

Practice the listening skills in Lifetime Tool 6. Listen carefully to what the panelists are trying to tell you. Draw out the feelings behind the words.

Close the panel by again thanking the panelists for their business and participation.

Provide a small token of your appreciation. For example, a client of mine gave away a handsome desk clock with his company's name on the base.

Treat everyone to lunch or dinner. Make it a casual setting where participants can get to know one another better.

Following Up After the Panel

Holding the panel is not enough. You need to share the information you've gained and implement the suggestions you decide to adopt.

Analyze and share client feedback.

After the panelists have departed, discuss and analyze with your team the panelists' comments. Develop a list of all client suggestions. Rank them in importance. Don't skip this part of the process. Sometimes, it's the most important.

Send personal thank-you notes to all panelists. The notes can come from the president of the firm or from the person who handles the particular panelist's account. In your note, acknowledge a panelist's particularly significant comment.

As soon as possible, get to work implementing the suggestions from your clients. An idea delayed may be an idea denied.

Have some sort of newsletter, e-mail or other mechanism for communicating the results of the panel to the participants and clients. Describe the panel and tell all your clients specifically what you learned and what you are doing about it. Encourage additional and ongoing client feedback.

Continue to update all your clients on what you've done as a result of the panel. Make your clients aware of what has been implemented. If something has not been implemented, tell them that, too, and explain why.

Consider forming an advisory board consisting of panelists who contributed the most, and schedule either quarterly or semiannual meetings.

When you consider a major company decision, enlist the advisory board. After all, if your clients are the most important part of your business, doesn't getting their advice on major decisions make sense?

Hold another panel with different panelists in 12 months to get more input from diverse sources.

Get client feedback, and get it often.

Keep the client lines of communication open. You need not have a panel to get good feedback. If you have done your job well, clients should be encouraged to call you and offer feedback.

Recognize that your most profitable ideas will come from either your associates or your clients.

QUESTION FOR YOU

- *What mechanism do you have in place to capture this valuable client feedback?*

Client Survey Forms

Besides panels, another way to gain valuable client feedback is by developing and distributing a client survey form. Whether you have one client or 100,000 clients, you need their ongoing feedback to be successful and profitable.

How to Design a Useful Client Survey Form

The more carefully you design your client survey form, the more useful the results will be. Take a look at the two sample feedback forms on pages 196 and 197. I have included Ben & Jerry's®

because it is one of the best I have come across. It's simple, to the point, fun, and allows for general comments.

I have also included a generic hotel survey to give you an idea of what *not* to do. The form is too long, with too many questions. It's tedious and too exhausting to fill out—and most people won't.

Consider the following strategies when you design your form.

Tell your associates what they do well and how they can improve.

Use the form for feedback only, not for marketing. Decide that you are gaining client feedback only. These surveys should not be veiled marketing pieces. Feedback and marketing are two separate functions and should not be mixed. If you say a survey is for customer service purposes and then bombard clients with marketing questions, you insult your clients. You run the risk that clients will not fill out your survey and perhaps will be so offended that they never do business with you again.

Genuinely thank clients for their business. At the outset, thank clients for the opportunity to serve them. Be as respectful and grateful as you can. I have found that the more respectful and grateful you are in these surveys, the more clients will respond and the more honest the feedback you will receive. Honest client feedback is your ultimate goal.

Get your associates' input. If your company has many departments, enlist the aid of all your associates in developing the client-feedback survey. Input from shipping and receiving and technical support is just as important as input from sales and management. Ask your associates, "If you could ask your clients any question to improve our performance, what would you ask them?"

Getting associates' input is crucial in two regards: You will develop a better and more comprehensive survey form, and your associates will buy into the survey process. Because they helped design the form, they will want to see the results. Developing and sharing results from a client survey offers an excellent opportunity to build a stronger team. You share a common goal—exceeding clients' expectations—and you must work together as a team to reach your goal by developing a comprehensive client survey.

Provide as many avenues as possible for client feedback.

Pinpoint the exact areas in which you want feedback. You will receive one type of response when you ask a general question, "How is our service?" You will receive a more valuable response when you ask, "How was our service in sales, order fulfillment, customer service and accounting?" Or better yet, "How can we improve our service in each of these departments?"

One last caution: Do not go overboard on your survey. We have all seen hotel surveys that look like IRS forms. And I bet that because of the length of such surveys, you don't fill them out. Keep your survey simple.

Allow for and encourage general comments. Designate space for general comments. Such open comments can be worth a million dollars: "You know, it might help if you . . . ," or, "Your competition does a good job when . . ."

In short, in gaining client feedback, don't just have clients grade your performance; get hard and fast suggestions for improvement by providing space for them.

BEN & JERRY'S® SURVEY FORM

Thanks for visiting Ben&Jerry's®!

We want to know how you would rate the experience.

1. How was the ice cream or frozen yogurt?

☐ The Greatest ☐ Pretty Darn Good ☐ O.K.

2. Were you treated in a friendly and courteous manner?

Oh, Yes. ☐ No. ☐

Comments: ____________________

____

3. The store should be ship-shape and clean. Was it?

☐ Yes. ☐ No.

Squeek

Comments: ____________________

4. Did we have what you asked for?

☐ Yes, definitely. ☐ Unfortunately, Not.

Comments: ____________________

5. How would you rate your experience at Ben & Jerry's?

☐ Excellent! ☐ GOOD! ☐ FAIR ☐ POOR

Comments:

____

6. What can we do to improve your experience? ____________________

____________________ (Please continue on back of page...)

7. How often do you visit this shop?

☐ more than once a week ☐ once a week ☐ once a month

☐ less than once a month ☐ this is the first time

8. How far did you travel to get here? ____________________

Your Name: ____________________

Address: ____________________

____________________ Date:________ Time:_____ ☐ AM ☐ PM

Would you like to be on our mailing list? ☐ Yes. ☐ No.

Additional comments and suggestions can be written on the back of this page. Printed on Recycled Paper

Ben & Jerry's® Ice Cream

HOTEL SURVEY FORM

Room No.: ______
Date: ______
Dates: Arrival: ______ Departure: ______
Business or Pleasure: ______
Name: ______
Address: ______
______
Telephone: Home: ______ Bus.: ______
Company: ______

	Exceeded Expectations	Met Expectations	Did Not Meet Expectations
ARRIVAL			
Door Staff Greeting	❐	❐	❐
Front Entrance/ Lobby (appearance)	❐	❐	❐
Reception			
Luggage Service	❐	❐	❐
GUEST ROOM			
First Impression	❐	❐	❐
Housekeeping:			
Morning ❐	❐	❐	❐
Evening ❐	❐	❐	❐
Maintenance	❐	❐	❐
Amenities	❐	❐	❐
TELEPHONE SERVICE			
Manner	❐	❐	❐
Promptness	❐	❐	❐
Message Handling	❐	❐	❐
CONCIERGE			
Attitude	❐	❐	❐
Efficiency	❐	❐	❐
HEALTH CLUB			
Housekeeeping	❐	❐	❐
Maintenance	❐	❐	❐
Amenities	❐	❐	❐
Attitude of Staff	❐	❐	❐
NEWS/GIFT SHOP			
Promptness	❐	❐	❐
Quality of Product	❐	❐	❐
LAUNDRY/VALET			
Promptness	❐	❐	❐
Quality of Product	❐	❐	❐
Attitude of Staff	❐	❐	❐

	Exceeded Expectations	Met Expectations	Did Not Meet Expectations
BARS & RESTAURANTS			
Riverside Cafe:			
Quality of Food	❐	❐	❐
Quality of Service	❐	❐	❐
Attitude of Staff	❐	❐	❐
Lobby Lounge:			
Quality of Beverage	❐	❐	❐
Quality of Service	❐	❐	❐
Attitude of Staff	❐	❐	❐
Room Service:			
Promptness	❐	❐	❐
Quality of Food	❐	❐	❐
Quality of Service	❐	❐	❐
Attitude of Staff	❐	❐	❐
Banquets/Catering:			
Quality of Food	❐	❐	❐
Quality of Service	❐	❐	❐
Attitude of Staff	❐	❐	❐
Quality of Facilities	❐	❐	❐
DEPARTURE			
Cashier:			
Efficiency ❐	❐	❐	❐
Attitude of Staff ❐	❐	❐	❐
Bell Staff Services	❐	❐	❐
Door Staff	❐	❐	❐
Valet parking	❐	❐	❐

YOUR COMMENTS

______
______
______

Is there a service, facility or amenity you would like added? ______
______
______

Ask "will we have the opportunity to serve you again?" Always include this question at the end of your survey. It's a good idea to also ask, "Why or why not?" You need to know what you are doing well so that you can duplicate and continue to improve it. You also need to know what you need to improve.

The determining question for you is always "Will this client return?" That's what ultimately matters. They may be upset about this or that, but the bottom line is, "Are they returning?"

Post a survey on your Web site. For immediate feedback, e-mail it to your clients.

Make your survey easy to fill out and return. The easier your feedback form is to fill out, the greater your chances of getting responses. Be sure to include a stamped, self-addressed envelope so the form is easy to mail back. Don't make your clients hunt around for your address or have to buy a stamp to give you feedback. Your investment in postage will be paid over and over again by the feedback you receive. The information you gain from this survey will be incredibly valuable in helping you develop and maintain lifetime clients.

Also designate one person to receive the forms. Clients feel more comfortable when they see an individual's name on the return address.

Other questions to ask. Depending on your business, you want to ask specific and directed questions to gauge the quality of your service. In essence, you want to ask clients:

- **Did we do what we said we would do?**
- **Did we exceed your expectations?**
- **What other services might we provide for you?**

Again, keep the survey brief and to the point.

The easier it is to fill out, the better the odds that clients will fill it out.

TRUE STORY: Gathering Client Feedback—Do You Just Get a 10, or Do You Earn It?

Recently, I completed a simple transaction with a major bank. At 3:00 P.M. on Friday, the lobby was closed. I had to go through the bank's drive-through. The cars were waiting three to four deep in line on a hot day. When I completed the transaction, I found this message on the bank receipt: "Our goal is to provide you with excellent customer service. Please award us a '10' rating if you are called."

In surveying clients, don't just have them grade your performance; solicit their specific suggestions for improvement.

I was impressed that the bank was surveying its customers, but I wasn't impressed with its request. The bank appeared to ask its customers to "just award us a 10" as a gift without any hard work on its part.

You do not earn lifetime clients by asking people to give you a 10. You earn lifetime clients by asking how you can improve and then by implementing the suggestions. Nowhere on that form did the bank give me an opportunity to tell it how it could improve. And to date, I have not received a customer service call from either the bank or a company hired by it to assess its service.

As it happened, I had just come from another bank across the street whose air-conditioned lobby had been open Friday at 3:00 P.M. There were no lines. I had walked straight to a teller window, received a friendly hello, completed my transaction and was out the door, all in less than a minute. Which bank do you think has a greater opportunity to earn my lifetime business?

Moral of the story: You must earn lifetime clients by always asking, "How can we improve our service to you?"

TRUE STORY: No Feedback Form, No Repeat or Referral Business

Share client feedback with all your associates.

The book you are now holding has gone through many generations. At one point, I photocopied 30 manuscripts, each more than 200 pages, and sent them out to clients and associates all over the country for their feedback.

The print shop that did the photocopying did an OK job. I say just "OK" because, after sending out the 30 manuscripts, I found that four or five pages from the original manuscript were missing from each copy.

The print shop provided no feedback form for me to fill out to make the shop aware of the problem and suggest improvements. I was too busy to pick up the telephone and advise the shop of the missing pages. Besides, how many people want to make a call like this? Yet I would think the print shop would want to know of this problem.

I spent approximately $500 for these 30 bound copies. If all the pages had been there, I definitely would have used the shop's services again. My company probably does $5,000 in photocopying a year. So, because of some mishap—which could have been a machine malfunction or a human error—the shop missed out on the opportunity for $4,500 in additional business and any referral business I might have sent its way.

Lastly, because the print shop has no feedback form, it will not be able to avert the mistake for future clients. Along with losing my business, how much other potential business will it lose?

The moral of this story is that to keep clients for life, you must get client feedback on the quality of your service.

Other Ways to Get Client Feedback

In addition to client panels and survey forms, you have other options available for collecting feedback, including the following:

Share client feedback in graphic forms that everyone will understand.

Interviews

Interview clients either on the telephone or in person after the product or service is delivered.

You may get an objective third party to ask the questions. If you do, however, be aware that what you gain in objectivity, you may lose in having an interviewer who doesn't know your company as well as you do. Whoever does this type of telephone surveying needs to be aware of all the nuances of your businesses. In addition, when you contact your clients through a third party, you may lose valuable insights in the process of gathering and analyzing the information.

Conversely, all clients must feel comfortable sharing their experiences. You will receive one level of feedback by having a person involved with your business do the interviewing and a different level of feedback by having an objective third party call.

Toll-free Suggestion Line

Offer and thoroughly advertise a telephone number that your clients or anyone in your organization can call at any time, day or night, to voice their opinions and offer suggestions for improvement.

Again, make sure you have a system in place to capture, analyze and share all the valuable feedback you receive. To have the telephone line and not do anything with the information would be a waste. In fact, you are better off not having the line at all than giving your clients and associates the appearance that you don't value their feedback.

When you continually improve, your most demanding clients become your best advocates.

List and post all suggestions, and reward the best ones.

TRUE STORY: Tropicana—A Toll-Free Number Really Does Work

Recently, I purchased a 10-ounce Tropicana orange juice from a local bagel shop. For the second time in a row, I had an extremely difficult time opening the carton.

On the carton I found a toll-free number for "Questions or Comments." I called the number and spoke with a customer service rep named Barbara Sullivan. After I explained my problem, the first thing Barbara did was to thank me for "taking the time to call." Barbara informed me sincerely that hearing from callers like me was "the only way we can do our job better." Next Barbara asked me:

"At what store did you buy the two cartons?"

"Do you still have the carton that prompted the call?"

"What is the date and code across the top?"

Barbara then explained to me that Tropicana uses more than one glue to seal its cartons. Perhaps there had been a mix-up in the batches. She apologized for the inconvenience this had caused me. She then asked if she could send me something. A couple of days later I found in the

LETTER FROM TROPICANA

Tropicana®

May 7, 1999

Mr. Rick Buckingham
6610 Rockledge Drive
Bethesda, MD 20817

Dear Mr. Buckingham:

Thank you for contacting us about your experience with Tropicana Pure Premium Orange Juice. It is important for us to know when a consumer is dissatisfied with one of our products.

Our containers must be sealed properly to assure freshness and quality. We also know that packages must be convenient for consumer use and we regret that it was difficult for you to open.

Consumer input is very important to us. We are continually evaluating our products and packaging, and your comments will be forwarded to the proper departments for their review.

We appreciate having this brought to our attention and apologize for any inconvenience this has caused you. I have enclosed some coupons and hope you'll try our product again.

Sincerely,

Barbara Sullivan
Coordinator
Consumer Relations Department

ABS/CAA

Enclosures

0566241A

Tropicana Products, Inc. Consumer Relations P.O. Box 338, Bradenton, Florida 34206
800•237•7799

mail a letter (see page 203) and coupons.

Given the service, courtesy, and a sincere desire to improve their operations, do you think I will continue to buy Tropicana products?

Random Telephone Surveys

Reward the best staff suggestions.

Hire either a third party or an objective and polite individual in your organization to call clients randomly using a short feedback form. Do not make the telephone calls too long and, again, don't use them as veiled marketing opportunities. Use the calls as an opportunity to survey your clients about how you can improve your services.

E-Mail and Web Site

A hassle-free and effective way to gain feedback is through the Internet. You can post a blank survey on your Web site and ask for input. You can also e-mail your clients asking for feedback.

What to Do With the Feedback You Get

No matter what mechanism you use to get client feedback, you need to do the following with the information you collect:

Properly Analyze the Data

The information you collect from your feedback mechanisms will be useless unless you analyze it. In the case of client surveys, you need to compare the number of surveys you sent out with the number returned to ensure that you have a valid sample. Then tally the responses to each question and determine the percentage of responses that are the same. For example, what percentage of respondents told you your accounting department's service exceeded their expectations—25 percent? 85 percent?

Share the Information

Form a client advisory board. Solicit its input on major business decisions.

Make sure everyone in your organization sees the results of feedback you've collected. It does no good to develop a survey or create a client panel unless you share the results with your associates. You won't improve your organization until everyone sees the results of his or her performance. Good places to share these results include in the company newsletter, on the company Web site, intranet and screensavers, and in prominent spots throughout the workplace.

Share the results with your clients. After all, you have asked them for their input. More important, sharing with your clients puts you on notice. Now everyone knows what needs to be done.

Be creative in how you share the results. Don't just show numeric listings. I recommend developing color bar graphs and pie charts, and posting them for everyone to see. Make sure to walk workers through the results so they understand the information they are seeing.

Implement Suggested Improvements

You need to begin to implement the suggestions your clients make. Let your clients know what improvements you've implemented as a result of their suggestions. Knowing that you value their suggestions enough to implement them will make your clients feel more like they're in a partnership with you and that you're interested in constantly improving your service.

Continually Improve and Update Your Feedback Mechanism

The sooner you get client feedback, the sooner you will improve.

If you are not getting the number of responses you want, improve your feedback mechanism. You should always be developing better, more precise questions to ask.

For written surveys, I recommend including at the bottom of the form who developed the form and the date and year it was developed. If the form has had revisions, you should note this, including date, year and who did the revisions.

Consider Rewarding Clients for Input

I am somewhat reluctant to say this, but here it is: Consider rewarding clients for their input. The main point here is not to get hung up on giving clients presents. The main point is to respectfully gain clients' input on how to improve service and then implement it. Do not lose the focus on gaining valuable feedback.

After you have implemented their suggestions or told them why you can't, consider some sort of more specific reward for their suggestions. It might be a discount on future products and service.

The best way you can reward and thank clients for their input is to do all you can do to implement the suggestions they have shared. When you are successful in doing that, both you and your clients win.

THINGS TO DO "MONDAY MORNING"

- **Always ask clients,** "How are we doing?" "How can we improve?
- **Be specific in requesting client feedback.** What you ask for, you will get.
- **At the close of a project,** ask clients for their suggestions for future improvements.
- **In written surveys,** allow for clients' general comments.
- **Analyze and share the results** with clients and associates.
- **Implement clients' improvement suggestions.**

Converting Complaining Clients Into Lifetime Clients

LIFETIME TOOL

10

CUSTOMER ONCE, CLIENT FOREVER

In this chapter, I'll share:

- **The impact and opportunities of clients' complaints on your business**
- **The cost of not responding to complaints**
- **Why no news from clients is not necessarily good news**
- **Why clients leave**
- **How to turn angry clients into loyal, lifetime clients**
- **Other strategies to win back lost clients**

Most businesspeople shy away from dealing with complaints. They mistakenly believe that ignoring complaints is a whole lot easier than facing them head-on and fixing the problems. They label complaining clients as difficult, unreasonable or complainers without taking time to hear what these people are saying.

I speak from experience because I did the same thing. I would avoid upset clients, and deny or simply dismiss their grievances: "Boy, what a pain in the neck." I soon learned that I was missing some valuable opportunities. I will share a story on page 212 that explains the transformation in my thinking: how I stopped resenting customer complaints and began valuing client input.

As the statistics in this chapter (taken from W. Edwards Deming's book *Out of the Crisis* and Laura Liswood's book *Serving Them Right*) show, if you continue to ignore complaints, the problems may not go away, but your clients surely will. You must learn to embrace complaints, to see them as opportunities to better serve clients instead of merely as problems to fix.

TRUE STORY: The Wisdom of Youth

A couple of years ago, I presented a workshop for a successful financial-services company that processed an extremely high number of transactions. The firm was in constant contact with clients, and sometimes these clients would get very anxious about their transactions.

When we reached the part of the workshop that dealt specifically with customer service, everyone wanted to talk. Initially, seasoned customer service people spoke of all the challenges of serving what can be extremely demanding clients—"Clients want this and want that." What I heard from these experienced people was how difficult and demanding clients could be.

Realize that complaints are excellent opportunities to gain lifetime clients.

After several comments like this, a young woman raised her hand and, acknowledging these remarks, said that such calls did not unnerve her. She looked at these demanding client calls as an opportunity to build a "lifetime partnership" (her words) with these clients. The young woman maintained that the more upset the client, the greater the opportunity to have a lifetime partnership with him or her. She would simply let clients speak first, then walk them through what needed to be done and allay their fears. There was silence in the room after she spoke.

I asked how old she was. She said 24. I told her that with her attitude she would have great success in business. The older, more seasoned people had not seen what this young woman had seen. The demanding clients were, in effect, not to be avoided. The demanding clients represented an opportunity for lifetime relationships.

QUESTIONS FOR YOU

- *Do you view complaints as an opportunity to develop a lifetime partnership with your clients?*
- *Do you avoid demanding clients, or do you seek to forge a deeper partnership with them?*

The Impact of Client Complaints

A client tells eight to ten people about a positive sales experience; he or she tells 16 to 18 people about a negative sales experience.

We learn something very simple here. Clients have a much greater tendency to complain than to brag about good service. In effect, if you do a good job, a client will tell others. If you do a bad job, a client will tell close to twice as many people.

Seemingly annoying calls from past clients now become excellent new business opportunities.

The better the job you do, the more free advertising you will get. Doing a bad job, however, can get you just as much bad advertising. If for some reason you do a bad job, do whatever it takes to fix it. In alienating one client, you are in effect alienating at least 16 potential clients. This ripple effect should motivate you enough to exceed all your clients' expectations.

If you are not motivated by pride to do good work, be motivated by the possibility of getting negative advertising. You don't want clients out there spreading bad comments about you and your performance.

When you do receive complaints, do everything you can to address and solve the clients' concerns. If you are not doing so already, begin to look at complaints as an opportunity to improve your business and earn a lifetime client. Let me share the story I mentioned at the outset of this chapter that taught me how to deal with complaints.

QUESTIONS FOR YOU

- *What are your clients saying about the quality of your service?*
- *How many of your clients would say that*

they have had a positive experience with you? How many a negative experience?

TRUE STORY: Complaints Are Really Opportunities

Do whatever it takes to keep clients happy.

The Rouse Co. is a national developer located in Columbia, Md. Ten years ago, I had the opportunity to do a medium-size project ($15,000) for Randy Byrd, the head of the company's purchasing department.

When my company went to install the product, we had four or five minor problems—nothing major, but enough to cause concern. Randy was called to the site, and he phoned me from the site to advise me of the situation. He wanted me on the site immediately.

I was in the middle of preparing a bid on another project. At 3:00 in the afternoon, the last thing I wanted to do was to make an unplanned, 90-minute-round-trip site visit. So I began to "double talk." I wanted to get Randy off the telephone. Randy picked up on this and said, "Rick, come out and see me." I sensed Randy's concern and his urgency. I reluctantly agreed and said, "I will be right there."

So I closed the bid that I was working on, knowing I would have to give up on that project and grudgingly got in my car for a 45-minute trip to Columbia. All I could think about was "lost-opportunity cost"; the proposal I was working on might have led to another sale, another client. Going to see Randy also meant additional costs to the project. I also was sure the appointment would carry over to the evening. The last thing I wanted to do that afternoon was to drive 45 minutes to deal with a complaining customer. It turned out to be the best thing I would do.

As I drove up the road, my attitude started to soften a bit. I realized a few things:

- **Randy had given me an opportunity to bid on a $15,000 project,** a nice-sized contract.
- **He had awarded my company the contract quickly.**
- **Randy hadn't beaten me up on the price.** He signed our proposal and sent it back. In an extremely competitive industry, this was uncommon. In short, I had a $15,000 project at the price I wanted it.
- **Randy had always been polite and professional.** I owed him the same in return.
- **All signs said that I couldn't afford to treat Randy like a one-time customer;** this was the kind of client we'd like to do business with in the future. I couldn't afford to lose this client at installation.

Properly solving clients' complaints will pay future dividends.

By the time I met with Randy, my disposition was a lot better. I was not thinking about lost-opportunity cost, wear and tear on my car, or being in Columbia late one afternoon. I was thinking I needed to do all within my power to make him happy. I gave Randy my undivided attention.

We spent a half-hour walking the site. I came to admire Randy a great deal because he was very thorough. He explained all his concerns, point by point. I took notes. After the site tour, Randy said he had to run to another meeting but wanted me to update him on what needed to be done.

I met with our installer, and by that evening we had all the kinks worked out. As instructed, I called Randy's voice mail that evening and left a detailed message about what was done and what needed to be done. By the next day, everything had been squared away and Randy was pleased with both our work and our response to his telephone call.

About two weeks later, I received a call from one of Randy's associates that led to another sale. And a month after that, I received another referral call from Randy that also led to a sale. I learned an incredibly valuable lesson: Spending that afternoon completely satisfying (and ultimately exceeding the expectations of) my existing client was much more important and profitable than pursuing a new client.

It's clients' perception of your service, not your perception, that ultimately matters.

If I had not gone out to see Randy and handle what ended up being minor details, I would have missed an excellent opportunity to develop a lifetime client. Randy's precision encouraged me to be more precise. In addition, by handling Randy's complaint I developed a higher comfort level dealing with clients because I had a much clearer picture of what Randy wanted and what future clients were likely to want.

In the end, many people were positively affected by this experience:

- **Randy was happy** because we satisfied his immediate needs. What could have been a negative experience turned out to be a positive one.
- **Our installer was happy** because we responded to the issues quickly. He wasn't left hanging. He was able to finish the project and move on.
- **My accounting department was happy** because, after responding quickly, we were also paid quickly.
- **Perhaps I gained the most from the experience.** I left the project with a greater confidence and awareness of how to serve clients and a much greater sense of pride in my work. While at first I did not want to see Randy, it turned out to be the best thing I could have done.

After the experience with Randy, I approached every customer service call with a greater confidence in my ability to exceed my clients' expectations. I also overcame any fear of a "complaining" client. Each complaint was an opportunity. I realized the best thing for me to do was not to avoid a complaint but to embrace it as an opportunity to improve my service.

Always maintain a meaningful dialogue with clients.

QUESTIONS FOR YOU

- *Are you embracing complaints? If not, what holds you back?*
- *When was the last time you pursued a complaining client?*

No News Is Not Necessarily Good News

For every client who complains, 26 will instead quietly take their business elsewhere. From Laura Liswood's book, we learn that one study in the banking industry documented that one complaint letter equaled 26 lost clients. While that one person took the time to write about a problem, 26 simply took their business elsewhere.

Most people never take the time to officially complain. Just because you don't hear from a client doesn't mean everything is fine. You should be concerned about clients who complain, but you should be even more concerned about clients you don't hear from. That's why it's crucial to get ongoing client feedback.

In workshops, I remind people that no news is not necessarily good news! If you have not heard from clients in a couple of weeks, pick up the telephone and call, or better yet, drop by and say hello: "How are you doing? How has our service been? How can we serve you better?" You want honest feedback from clients.

By the way, if you worked in the banking industry and and received that one complaint, how would you respond? I often hear a variety of responses. Later I'll share a story of a Staples office manager who received a complaint letter and turned it into a lifetime-client opportunity.

Most lifetime clients are won or lost in the unexpected moments.

For now, recognize that complaining clients are really offering you an opportunity to keep their business. They want to see what you are going to do with the complaint.

TRUE STORY: It's the Information You Don't Get That Can Hurt You

In Lifetime Tool 2, Properly Preparing Yourself to Win the Lifetime Relationship, I mentioned the training program we presented for the customer service department of a waste-management company. Its market was extremely competitive and price sensitive.

One customer service representative in the program told of a client who called her to learn more about the firm. He was ready to go with a competitor but had wanted to make one last call to complete his research. Evelyn had a nice conversation with this potential client—so nice, in fact, that the client was just about ready to sign with her when he said he wanted to check one last fact with the competitor.

The client hung up and called the competitor. The telephone rang four times without being answered. He hung up, called Evelyn back, and started service with her immediately, saying that if the competing firm could not answer its telephone properly, how could it serve him properly?

This story has two morals: First, the competitor lost the chance to get the business because no one answered the telephone quickly enough. More important, the competitor will never know that it lost the business and why it lost the business. How much future business will it lose because no one answered the telephone quickly enough?

For better or worse, your clients are your best advertising resource. You have the choice: You can have them cursing you at a cocktail party or singing your praises and encouraging others to use your services. The choice is yours.

Immediately and personally solve clients' complaints.

QUESTIONS FOR YOU

- *Are you answering your telephone by the first or second ring?*
- *What clients haven't called you because they heard your service was lacking? How much does this represent in dollars?*

The Cost of Not Responding to Complaints

It costs anywhere from seven to 14 times more to get a new client than it does to retain an existing one. Why pay more to get a new client? Why not keep the ones you have? It's less expensive.

Most companies never bother to calculate what it costs for them to secure a client. They think they're making money by "churning" clients—that is, losing old clients and bringing in new ones. These companies believe new clients will always be available to draw from. They fail to take into account the cost of obtaining these new clients.

In my introduction ("Understanding the Philosophy of Lifetime Clients"), I discussed the value of lifetime clients and the cost of not keeping clients for life. The bottom line is that keeping clients is a lot more profitable than having to constantly attract new ones. The added cost of procuring new clients eats into your profit. Remember, it's not the gross sales you make but the profit you make that ultimately matters. Let me share a story of how keeping a client led to more than half a million dollars of profitable new business.

Take pride in converting complaining clients into lifetime clients.

TRUE STORY: Giving a Little, Gaining a Lifetime Client

I once had a client ask me to absorb an $800 invoice on a $30,000 project. Depending on how you looked at, either party could have been responsible for the $800. In the client's favor, the project had been delayed and was over budget. On our side, we had done everything the client told us to do. In short, one could have argued either side successfully.

Technically, I could have insisted the client pay the $800 invoice. I probably would have been paid, but most likely also would have lost the client's future business and any possible referral business.

My client asked me very honestly and directly if I could "make the $800 invoice disappear." He told me the project was way over budget and he would "take care of me down the road." While I was initially reluctant to do this, I weighed my doubts against the opportunity to do future business with him. I knew he had two or three projects coming up in the next six months. I could also sense the sincerity in his voice. So my company absorbed the invoice.

Over the next two years, this client happily sent us half a million dollars worth of business.

Please be careful interpreting what I'm saying. I'm not suggesting you "give away the store." What I am suggesting is that you weigh your options very carefully. In resolving client issues, consider the possibility of future business. The $800 we absorbed (a true cost of about $400) was an investment. If I had fought an $800 invoice, we probably would never have seen the half-million dollars of business we subsequently gained.

Price is not always a client's first concern.

QUESTIONS FOR YOU

- *What does it cost you to obtain a new client?*
- *Are you maximizing all your present opportunities with existing clients?*

Why Do Clients Leave?

A *U.S. News and World Report* study indicates that more than two-thirds of the people who stop buying from a particular company do so because they "perceive" that its employees are indifferent toward their needs and concerns. What this study says is that money is not what's most important. How clients are treated (service) is what ultimately matters. Knowing that price is often not the primary concern of clients, and that service is, is a key principle in developing lifetime clients.

Businesspeople who believe money is the primary concern of their clients project that belief so much that, in their minds, it becomes a reality.

If a client does leave on the basis of price, you need to ask yourself whether you want that person as a lifetime client. My experience is that there are plenty of clients out there who are more concerned with excellent service than the price of a product or service. You don't need to hang on to those for whom price is everything. By working smart and diligently, and applying the strategies discussed in this book, you will find the service-first clients.

You don't make money "churning" clients. You make money keeping clients for life.

I've emphasized the word "perceived" above because, as I've said before, what ultimately matters is not whether you think you did a good job but whether your client thinks so. It's your client's perception of the service, not yours, that ultimately matters. When you make this shift and look at your performance through your client's eyes, you will take a major step toward developing lifetime client relationships.

QUESTIONS FOR YOU

- *Have you worked on transactions that you thought went well but the client thought did not go well?*
- *Conversely, have you worked on transactions you thought did not go well and the client thought went well?*

Strategies for Turning Angry Clients Into Loyal, Lifetime Clients

Can you retain clients who complain? Absolutely! Most lifetime relationships are won or lost on the basis of how you respond to complaints.

Most businesspeople mistakenly believe that the critical point in developing a relationship with a client is the early stage—when all the wining and dining and getting to know each other occurs. Actually, the critical steps that determine the life span of the relationship are all the unexpected events that occur later. Clients watch how you handle their complaints, how you deal with them when they are upset. By using the following strategies, you can turn your most irate clients into loyal, lifetime clients.

Demanding clients will go out of their way to reward good service.

Generously Listen to Clients' Concerns

Just as we discussed in Lifetime Tool 6, listen to clients. Don't interrupt. Let clients talk. Hear them out completely. Let them vent. Don't let clients go overboard, but let them express all their feelings. Until they get their anger and frustration out, they will be hard to deal with. (Review all the listening strategies from Lifetime Tool 6, Hearing What Your Clients Are Actually Saying, if you need to.)

Listen specifically to a client's tone of voice; that usually tells you how angry your client is. Your goal is to relax the client. As your client is speaking he or she should be calming down, not getting angrier. The client's tone of voice should be a good barometer of how you are doing.

While clients are upset, recognize and remember that they are not upset with you; they are upset with the situation—with not getting complete satisfaction. Plus, a client might just be having a bad day.

Whatever the reason, you will be more effective dealing with a challenging client when you do not take a complaint personally. Keep your angriest clients focused on the facts and on your desire to help them.

After clients have told you why they are upset, thank them for sharing their concerns with you. A thank-you acknowledges that you've heard what clients have said.

TRUE STORY: Defusing Angry Clients

Clients' tone of voice is a good barometer of how they feel. Listen to it.

I once led a workshop for the customer service department of a large insurance company. We were discussing the importance of listening to clients and letting them express their feelings.

I noticed a woman who had been quiet and shy for most of the workshop who suddenly began to smile. I asked her to share with us what she was smiling about. She proceeded to tell a story about an irate client who had called her. The upset client talked heatedly for three or four minutes while the customer service representative patiently listened.

Then the customer stopped talking, paused and began to apologize to the customer service representative. The client said she had had a bad day and apologized for taking it out on the customer service rep.

Because of this experience and, in particular, the customer service representative's patience, the company and the client have since developed a close business relationship. In fact, the woman has become one of the firm's better clients.

The key here was that the customer service rep let her client express her feelings. She did not argue with the client; she patiently listened.

Apologize and Empathize

How would you handle the one angry client out of 26 who took the time to write you? Some people in workshops suggest informing the boss or writing a response letter. If you took the time to write a letter, how do you want to be responded to? The best response is a simple telephone call. After all, if you wrote the letter, wouldn't you want a personal and immediate response?

After you have completely listened to and thanked the client for bringing this issue to your attention, genuinely apologize for whatever went wrong. Even when the problem is not your fault, give the client the benefit of the doubt and apologize. If the fault lies elsewhere in your company, assume responsibility anyway. The last thing an upset client wants to hear is about internal company issues. A genuine apology goes a long way toward soothing a disgruntled client, and soothing a disgruntled client will lead to your keeping that client for life.

It's not what you say, it's how you say it.

After you have listened and apologized to your client, empathize with him or her. Let your client know that you appreciate how he or she feels, that you understand. This should not be shallow or disingenuous. It must be sincere.

If you run a rental-car agency and a client's rental car has broken down in rush-hour traffic, you just don't say, "Oh, that happens." You can imagine the client's reaction. You will get a completely different reaction if you say something like, "We're so sorry that happened. We'll be right out to pick you up. What else can we do for you?"

QUESTIONS FOR YOU

- *Did you take your last client complaint call personally?*
- *Are you properly empathizing with your clients and their problems?*

Fix the Problem or Offer Restitution

If you resolve a problem on the spot, 95 percent of clients will stay.

If complaints are handled to a client's satisfaction, 90 percent of *upset* clients will stay.

The end of the rental car story hints at your last step of handling client complaints: Fix the problem—and the sooner the better.

Service matters more than price to lifetime clients.

If you truly want lifetime clients, apologies are not enough. You have to fix the problem that is the source of the complaint or, if you can't fix it, make up for the client's trouble in some other way.

Offer another, more expensive product if the product you've delivered is faulty and can't be replaced. Offer some free service in the future if slow or faulty service caused problems for the client that can't be fixed. Better yet, if clients don't like your proposed game plan, ask them, "What can we do to make this better?" In my experience, unhappy clients will invariably ask for less than you are willing to give them.

Now let's share how the Staples office manager handled a client complaint letter.

QUESTION FOR YOU

- *Are you proactively solving client concerns?*

TRUE STORY: How I Became a Loyal Staples Client

A couple of years ago, I went to my local Staples to buy office supplies. Over the past several visits, I had been frustrated by what I perceived as a lack of customer service.

On this trip, things happened that made me decide I was not going to shop there anymore. It was right around the holidays, and I debated whether I should write the manager and relate my experiences and my decision not to return. I decided that if I were the manager, I would want to know when someone was unhappy with my company's service, so I wrote a brief letter and did not think much of it. I never expected a reply.

Two days later, on a Sunday afternoon, during a football playoff game, I received a telephone call from the manager of Staples. He had received and read my letter. I was surprised to receive an acknowledgment, especially so quickly. The next two events surprised me even more.

Thank clients for complaining; they're telling you what to improve.

The store manager thanked me for writing and apologized for the substandard service.

Then he asked me a question that knocked me off my feet: "What can we do to make this up to you, Mr. Buckingham?"

While I was impressed by his call, my attention was still focused on the football game, so I was not sure how to answer. That prompted him to ask whether a $20 gift certificate would make it up to me. The manager mistook my distraction for indifference to his $20 offer and asked whether a $40 certificate would make it up to me. Obviously, I accepted the $40 certificate. The manager also told me that if I had any problems in the future, I was to ask for him and he would see to it that I was properly taken care of. I have been shopping there ever since.

For Staples, the $40 gift certificate has more than paid for itself. In addition to giving Staples my repeat business—my company probably spends $2,500 there annually—I have shared this story in numerous workshops and even in this book. The manager had no idea that his simple telephone call on a Sunday afternoon would lead to so much free advertising.

QUESTION FOR YOU

- *What clients do you have that, with a telephone call or visit like the one described above, could become lifetime clients?*

In Closing

Empathize with your clients.

Thank clients for taking time to call you and make you aware of how you can serve them better. Take control of the situation, and ask if your clients need anything else. Let your clients know that you are always available to them. If you are a customer service representative in a large organization, restate your name at the end of a telephone call and encourage your client to call you personally the next time he or she needs anything.

More Strategies

Here are some other practical pointers for communicating with and resolving problems for unhappy clients.

Stay in Charge

When clients complain, remember who is in control. You determine what gets done and what does not get done. You are the boss. Be fair but be firm.

Present a game plan to show you have things under control. "I/we are going to do the following . . ." Then do exactly what you said you would do. Do whatever it takes to satisfy the client. The loyalty and repeat business are worth it.

Make sure your proposal satisfies your client. If not, do what the manager from Staples did so well—ask "what can we do to make it better?"

Asking clients for input on how you can improve the situation is also important. You might be surprised at how little a client asks for.

Be Professional

Be polite and businesslike. Don't be rude to clients, but don't be overly friendly. I have spoken at times with customer service representatives who were flirtatious and unprofessional. Always be professional. Don't use the clients' first names if you don't know them personally and they haven't given you permission to do so.

Always be a consummate business professional.

I find great success calling people "Mr." and "Ms." and saying "yes, sir" and "no, ma'am." I find that good manners do much to defuse client anger. In addition, it's not what you say as much as how you say it that ultimately matters. Treat your clients with the utmost respect. Be aware of your voice tone. Make sure that your tone is professional, polite, friendly and not off-putting.

If clients curse or get out of hand, remind them that you want to assist them and you can't help them when they are upset. If clients really get upset, suggest that it may not be a good time to talk and ask if you could call them back when it might be a better time to talk.

QUESTION FOR YOU

- *Are you courteous and professional with your clients?*

Appreciate How Good It Feels to Save a Relationship With a Client

Finally, recognize how good you feel when you are able to turn an angry client into a lifetime client.

This is one of the most important steps in the list. I didn't just wake up one morning and decide that I wanted lifetime clients. Frustration motivated me to realize the value of lifetime clients and then develop strategies to win them.

I continued to pursue lifetime clients because of the fulfillment I felt when I exceeded clients' needs. It gave me tremendous satisfaction when I turned one-time buyers into lifetime clients.

Track client complaints and eliminate root causes.

QUESTION FOR YOU

- *Are you aware of how you feel when you win a client back?*

Complaints Equal Opportunities

My business experience improved greatly when I changed my perception about complaints. I was less fulfilled in my job when I saw complaints as pesky, annoying things that my clients inflicted on me in an attempt to ruin my day. I found greater fulfillment, and my sales and profitability soared when I began to see complaints as one of these three things:

Cries for attention. Clients wanted my attention; they wanted to make sure that I was aware of them and their concerns. Their bark was always much worse than their bite.

Opportunities to improve my service. Almost every time someone complained to me, I found a better, more cost-effective way to serve clients. I find that 95 percent of people who complain have legitimate concerns.

Something I could use to my advantage. Most

companies fail to adequately exploit client suggestions, whether expressed positively or as a complaint. Embrace complaints; they will make you stronger.

QUESTIONS FOR YOU

- *How did you handle your last complaining client?*
- *Did you succeed in turning that person into a lifetime client?*
- *What will you do differently the next time you encounter a complaining client?*
- *Are you tracking what percentage of angry clients you save?*

When clients no longer call, find out why.

Strategies to Win Back "Lost" Clients

Be realistic. As much as I would like to tell you that you will win all your clients, you will not win them all for life, at least not on the first try. Some clients may leave. Just do the best you can.

Your goal is to always keep the door wide open so a client can freely return without any fear of rebuke or retribution. The client may suffer worse service elsewhere, want to come back, yet feel uncomfortable doing so. That would be a tragedy. Clients may come back in three hours, three weeks or three years. Always keep the door wide open and make it easy for them to return.

If, for whatever reason, you temporarily lose a client, don't give up. You can win clients back. To win back "lost" clients, use the strategies just discussed as well as the following suggestions:

Ask for Another Opportunity to Serve the Client

Ask your client to give you another shot on a new project. Do not be concerned with the size of the project; just ask for the opportunity. If you sense a client is reluctant to give you a second chance, ask for a small piece of business: "Let us have a small project to demonstrate our renewed commitment to you."

Recognize complaints as cries for attention from your clients.

Then do outstanding work with whatever size order or transaction a client gives you. Make especially sure that you correct whatever upset the client in the first place. If it was poor service, give your client excellent service. If you did not return calls in a timely enough fashion, return them as soon as possible. If you did not communicate well with the client, be in constant contact.

The bottom line is to show the client you have acknowledged what you did or failed to do and have mended your ways.

Your ultimate goal is to rebuild trust. Sometimes, you need to take small steps to rebuild that trust. Recognize this and act accordingly.

Be Pleasantly Persistent

Do not give up. Remember the lifetime value and all the referral opportunities you have. Your client may not accept your apology immediately. Stay in touch. The value of a client's repeat and referral business is well worth the effort.

As stated, it might take minutes, months, or even years for an upset client to return. You can't control when that will happen. You can only control your own behavior. Be polite and courteous. Keep the door wide open for a returning client.

Meanwhile, Seek Out Other Clients

If you are really distraught over losing a client, and have done all you could to win that client back, channel your remaining energy and seek out a new client to replace the one you lost. It's an abundant world, teeming with potential lifetime clients.

In the past, you may have denied or avoided complaining clients. With the strategies I have shared in this chapter, pursue these clients. Be aware that all the customer service statistics are heavily in your favor. Just the fact that you are acknowledging and responding to complaining clients is a step in the right direction.

Continually improving customer service is the best strategy for keeping clients for life.

QUESTIONS FOR YOU

- *Are you tracking the percentage of clients who return and continually trying to improve these figures?*
- *Which angry clients can you call today and win back?*
- *What changes will you make in your system to prevent losing future lifetime clients?*

(continued)

THINGS TO DO "MONDAY MORNING"

- **Address clients' complaints immediately.** They may become lifetime clients.
- **Empathize with clients;** let them know that you understand how they feel.
- **Ask complaining clients,** "What can we do to make it better for you?"
- **When a client does leave,** determine exactly why he or she is leaving and correct this for future clients.
- **Always keep the door wide open** for departed clients to return.

Properly Managing Your Client Base

LIFETIME TOOL

11

CUSTOMER ONCE, CLIENT FOREVER

In this chapter, I'll share:

- **GoalStar Lifetime Client Model**
- **How to determine the lifetime value of clients**
- **How to nurture existing relationships with clients**
- **What to do with clients that don't fit your business plan**

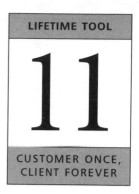

There are two strategies remaining in developing lifetime client relationships. In this chapter, I'll discuss how to maximize the relationships with your existing clients. I'll accomplish this by reviewing the GoalStar Lifetime Client Model and also by detailing how you can determine the lifetime value of a client. In the next chapter, I'll discuss how to develop your referral business.

I'm not saying here that you should rest on your client list and never look for new clients. No matter how happy you keep your clients, they may leave you for one reason or another—they could be bought by another company or may diversify into other fields, or your contact could leave. Keeping your eye out for new clients, especially those who can bring high-volume, high-profit projects to you, is always good business. However, while you are pursuing new clients, keeping all your existing clients for life is even better business.

Once you have established good relationships with clients and begin to feel that you will have them for life, you need to maintain these relationships.

You also need to know when and how to weed out clients that are not compatible with your business goals.

How Do Your Current Client Relationships Measure Up?

Do you know where you stand with your present clients? What percentage of their business are you winning? Are you offering your existing clients the complete range of your products and services?

Maximize all repeat and referral business opportunities with your clients.

TRUE STORY: Finding the Gold—Maximizing Your Current Client Relationships

A financial-services client called me and said he wanted to increase his sales. The previous year's sales were $30 million and he wanted a $10 million increase. He was convinced that $10 million would come from opening new accounts.

I thanked the client for the call and asked if I could spend some time with his people. I wanted to speak with his managers, salespeople, customer service representatives and clients. I wanted to get a clear sense of the client's business opportunities.

After three days of research, I found that my client could easily increase his sales by $10 million—not necessarily from new business but from his current clients. He did not have to go out and open any new accounts; he just needed to get more business from his existing accounts.

As I assessed the business, I realized that my client was getting only a percentage of his clients' business. The opportunity was not in opening new accounts but in maximizing the business opportunities with existing clients.

Before you start looking for new business,

take a look at the clients you already have. Determine where you stand with them—whether you're already getting all the business you can from those relationships. To help you, I've developed the GoalStar Lifetime Client Model and the GoalStar Lifetime Client Model Exercise, which follow.

QUESTION FOR YOU

- *Are you maximizing all business opportunities with existing clients?*

Make sure your clients' other divisions or sister companies are aware of all your services.

The GoalStar Lifetime Client Model

Kent Slepicka and I developed the GoalStar Lifetime Client Model to illustrate all the strategies I have been talking about.

EXPLANATION OF GOALSTAR LIFETIME CLIENT MODEL. There are three key points I want you to take away from this chart:

1. It describes the relationship between you and your clients. Recognize that your actions, those between you and your clients, do not take place in a vacuum. Clients respond to your actions. Just as you should size up clients, clients constantly size you up. They analyze your actions. The action verbs in the chart describe this businessperson-client relationship in detail. As you "analyze," "propose" and "perform," clients "evaluate," "accept" and "critique."

The first six tools in this book should assist you in making the sale. I've talked about strategies of properly serving clients, building client rapport, properly listening to clients and asking the right questions.

THE GOALSTAR LIFETIME CLIENT MODEL

This graph shows the process of achieving a lifetime client, which is a progression of 10 steps: your actions and your prospective customer's or client's corresponding reactions.

Note that your efforts won't begin to pay off until halfway through this process, at step 5, where you propose solutions and the customer accepts your proposal, thus earning you the initial sale.

But the last half of the journey will reward you, at every step of the way, with a closer, more satisfying and more profitable relationship with your client, culminating in a lifetime relationship. You'll find your greatest opportunities in steps 6 through 10.

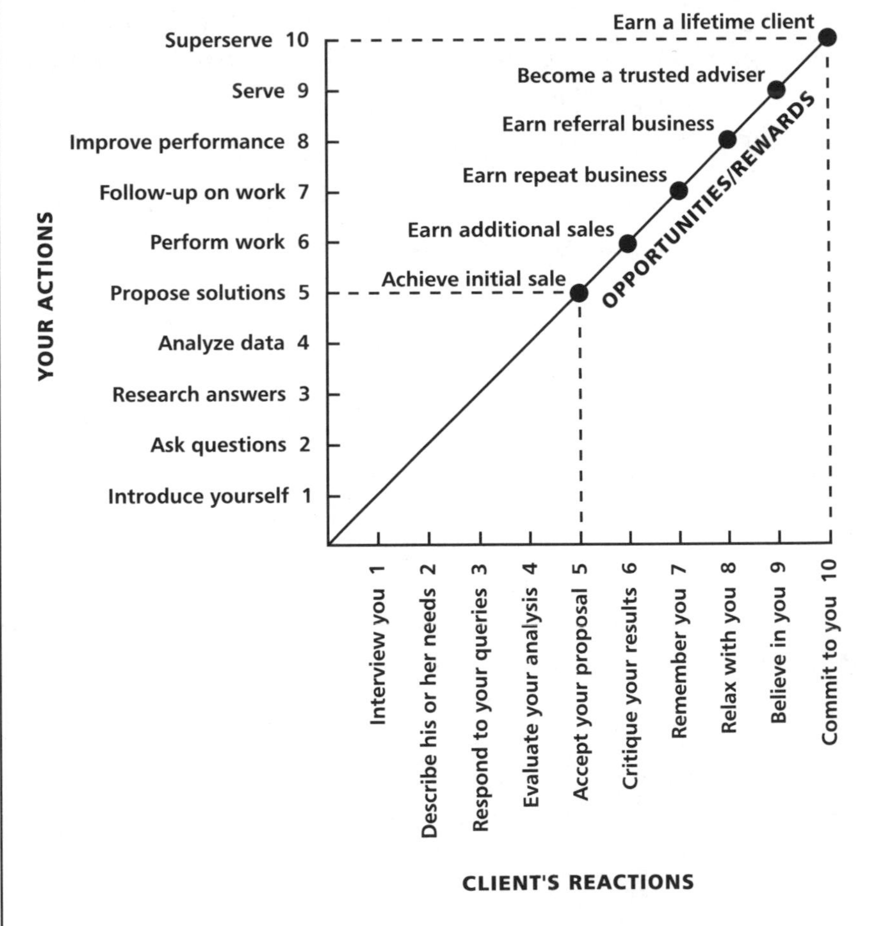

2. When you make a sale (at step 5), you are only halfway to a lifetime relationship. If you stop at the sale, you are missing out on untold opportunity. Unfortunately, most businesspeople today focus only on getting the sale. They mistakenly believe that when they make the sale, they have done all they need to do. These people neglect the opportunity for a lifetime client relationship.

An excellent opportunity to win lifetime clients lies in the order-fulfillment stage.

3. The greatest business opportunity exists after the sale (steps 6 and 10). When you make a sale, you have a satisfied client. But you don't want merely satisfied clients—you want loyal clients. Loyal clients will return, and they will refer others to you. Loyal clients make your job easier and more profitable.

GOALSTAR LIFETIME CLIENT MODEL EXERCISE

Stop reading right now, take out your client list, and pick five clients. List each client on the form and check off where you think you are in your relationship with that client. The next time you're in front of the client, verify where your relationship is. Then determine what steps are necessary to improve the client relationship. Implement these steps.

	CLIENT STATUS					
Client Name	Initial Sale	Additional Sales	Repeat Business	Referral Business	Trusted Adviser	Lifetime Client
1.						
2.						
3.						
4.						
5.						

Here's a critical point in understanding and developing lifetime clients. The steps on the chart between the sale, additional sale, repeat business and referral business are small steps. The most challenging work is getting the initial sale. With a little extra effort and the proper focus, you can achieve the additional sale and a client's repeat and referral business. Don't stop at the initial sale; lifetime clients offer you the greatest financial reward. I hope the True Story I shared on pages 212 to 215, "Complaints Are Really Opportunities," clearly demonstrates this point.

After you've sold clients, it doesn't take much effort to convert them into lifetime clients. Your financial returns will be exponential.

The second half of this book, Lifetime Tools 7 through 12, offers you specific strategies to gain loyal clients. I've discussed strategies to systemize your business to best serve your clients and maximize profits. I've shared numerous strategies for gaining valuable client feedback. I'll talk in the next chapter about how to maximize referral opportunities.

The next time you're in front of a client, confirm your GoalStar Lifetime Client Model rating by asking, "What percentage of your business are we getting? What can we do to earn more of your business?" You might be surprised at where your clients really are. By reading this book and implementing all the strategies, you should be able to move your clients to a 10 on the GoalStar Model, a lifetime partnership. You can use the form on page 237 to determine where you are with your clients.

QUESTIONS FOR YOU

- *Do you want just a sale or a lifetime client relationship?*
- *What percentage of your current clients are lifetime clients?*
- *How many marginally satisfied clients can you,*

with a telephone call and a plan of action, move to a 9 or 10 on the Lifetime Client Model?

- *How much more business will this bring in?*

TRUE STORY: Superserving Your Clients Pays Handsome Dividends

Determine exactly what a lifetime client is worth. Share the number with your entire organization.

Don't believe that your greatest business opportunities come from your existing clients? Read this story about George Hansen.

George sells commercial airtime for a radio station, an affiliate of a major media corporation, in Washington, D.C. A couple of years ago, George decided to superserve clients as his primary business strategy.

To implement this strategy, George identified those clients whom he couldn't serve well and referred them to his associates at the radio station. Having thus reduced his client list to 20 clients, he superserved them. Rather than just selling them airtime, George asked better questions and gained a deeper understanding of his clients' needs and ultimate goals. He appointed himself their unofficial "director of advertising." When George felt that his clients' needs would be better served elsewhere, he directed his clients' advertising dollars away from the radio station. George introduced his clients to high-quality people in related fields so that they could develop the best and most comprehensive advertising programs possible.

What were George's results? His clients were ecstatic, and his sales rose dramatically. George developed deeper, more profitable relationships with his 20 clients. He truly had become his clients' trusted adviser. George's clients were so happy that they referred more clients to him. George's business strategy was so successful that two years later, he reduced the number of his clients to just ten.

Analyze your client base. Determine which clients bring you the most profitable business.

Determining the Lifetime Value of a Client

Besides the GoalStar Lifetime Client Model, a second strategy to maximize your existing client base is to determine the dollar value of a lifetime client.

While it is difficult to put an exact dollar value on all the business lifetime clients will bring you, it helps to determine some sort of range of their worth. When I started to see my clients as $100,000 opportunities, I took client complaints more seriously. I saw that what I once thought were pesky, annoying client calls were really opportunities to build stronger and more profitable client relationships.

Determining the lifetime value of a client is not an exact science. I have worked with clients and come up with a value in the hundreds of thousands of dollars only to have that number shattered by million-dollar referral sales. I suggest that what matters here is not the actual figure you arrive at but the process you go through in arriving at a projected lifetime value.

Two things normally happen when you complete this exercise: You become even more aware of all your client repeat and referral opportunities, and you gain an even deeper respect for your current clients.

GoalStar Lifetime Client Example

Let's run through an example to demonstrate how this process works.

1. Determine the average dollar amount of a client's transaction. Let's say you bill $10,000 a year working on 50 transactions. Divide the total billings ($10,000) by the total number of transactions (50) for an average transaction of $200.

2. Determine how often this client will return for additional services over the course of a year, using any available data you may have or your best judgment. This is why it's a good idea to measure repeat business. Let's say a client returns on the average four times. Multiply average transactions ($200) by four, for $800.

3. Determine the number of times this client will refer you to others, again, using any data you have or your best judgment. This is why it's so important to ask clients, "How did you get our name?" On the average, let's say a client refers you five times. Multiply average transactions ($200) by 5, for $1,000.

4. Add all three figures together:

Initial transaction	$200
Repeat business	800
Referral business	+1,000
One-year value of client	$2,000

5. Multiply the final figure in step 4 by 10 for the ten-year average value of a lifetime client to you.

$2,000 x 10 years = $20,000 ten-year average value of a lifetime client

In this example, you took a single $200 transaction and turned it into a $20,000 lifetime client. If you look at all your clients in the same fashion, you will increase your sales exponentially.

Next time your telephone rings at 5:02 on Friday afternoon, remember that the caller is not a pesky client, but a potential lifetime client.

Seek to forge a deeper partnership with your clients.

QUESTION FOR YOU

- *What is a lifetime client worth to you?*

Maintaining Your Client Base

To maximize your opportunities with clients, you need to stay in touch and nurture the relationship. Don't make the mistake of taking clients for granted just because you seem to have a good working relationship. Building on the list from Lifetime Tool 4, page 87, here are some additional strategies to develop deeper client relationships.

Strategies to Nurture Existing Client Relationships

Think "lifetime partnership" from the moment you sit down with a client. Get an idea of how much business the company intends to do with your firm for the upcoming year. The actual dollar figure is not as important as the partnership process you will go through.

Always bring additional value to clients. Sit down and review your database and ask yourself how you can bring greater value to your clients. Which clients could be of mutual benefit to each other? Introduce them over the telephone or invite them both to lunch.

Develop a list of top clients, call, say hello, and ask these questions: "How are you doing?" "How's business?" "How can we help you be more successful?" I found success with a written client list complete with telephone numbers. As mentioned earlier, you can also input this information into a contact-management system and be prompted by your computer to call clients. How often you touch base depends on the nature of your business, but once a quarter is a good rule of thumb.

Provide business leads for your clients.

Provide e-mail updates. Keep them short, sweet and pertinent to a client's business. No one likes getting junk e-mail. Your e-mails could, for example, update clients on new services you offer.

When you're in the neighborhood, drop in and say hello. Leave your business card. Drop off bagels, cookies, tickets or movie passes. Let clients know you have been thinking of them and thank them again for the opportunity of working together.

Send your clients any news items that relate to their business. Don't automatically assume that your clients are aware of this information. Most times they are not. Always help your clients be more successful and profitable.

Look for any possible business to send a client. Make sure the person you are sending mentions your name when calling your client. Your clients will be pleasantly surprised when you actually refer business to them.

Create and mail a newsletter. Provide valuable information to clients. Keep your clients updated on current trends. Spotlight top projects. This keeps your name in front of a client.

Invite clients to lunch and thank them for their business. Ask how you can better serve them. Take clients who are not giving you much business to lunch and ask them specifically how you can better serve them or what holds them back from giving you more business. One of the best ways to build a lifetime relationship is by "breaking bread" with clients. When you take them to lunch, don't immediately talk about business unless your clients want to. Follow your clients' lead.

Creatively reward clients for their loyalty.

Know your clients' personal interests well enough that you can send articles or news clippings of personal interest: "I saw this in the newspaper and thought of you. Let me know if we can do anything for you."

Be alert for valuable people who may assist your clients. Whether it's a networking event, business dinner or social event, look for quality people who can contribute to your clients' efforts.

Your goal in business is to provide such outstanding service that you become an invaluable resource to your client. You want your clients to ask your advice and recommendations. When clients call and solicit your advice and ask for referrals, you've achieved success.

QUESTIONS FOR YOU

- *When was the last time you talked with your clients?*
- *Are all your clients aware of all your services?*

- *Have you referred clients to each other?*
- *Are you looking out for your clients' businesses and sending them information that would interest and benefit them?*

What to Do When Your Contact Leaves

Sometimes your contact in a client firm leaves. See this not as a setback but as an opportunity—actually two opportunities for new business.

Track and advise clients of their year-to-date spending with you.

First, find out what firm your former contact has joined to see if you can develop business there. If the person works in an industry that you can still serve, suggest a lunch or visit his or her new office to say hello.

Second, to maintain your relationship with the current client firm, ask your previous contact whom he recommends you speak with. Ask who will take over your contact's work. Call and introduce yourself to this new person. Depending on the business potential, a face-to-face meeting, lunch or coffee may be appropriate. Instead of losing an account, you now have two business opportunities to pursue.

Dealing With "Deadwood" Clients

People have asked on my workshop feedback forms, "How do you weed deadwood out of your client list—eliminate clients who do not give you enough business to make keeping them on your client list worthwhile?"

I always get concerned with questions like these because the question should not be, "How do you weed out deadwood business?" but rather, "Why do you think a client is deadwood?"

Refer lesser business to junior associates or smaller competitors.

Determining Whether Clients Are Deadwood

The first step is to determine whether you are maximizing your business opportunities with these clients. If you're not getting the majority of a client's business, why not? Once you establish the true business potential of a client, you're in a better position to assess an account. This assessment may very well show that some accounts are not worth keeping—that the time and energy you spend maintaining the account does not equal the business you're getting from it.

I'm always reluctant to get rid of clients. Maybe instead you can do something to increase the business you get from these underperforming clients. Even if seemingly deadwood clients do not have enough business to offer your firm, you still might get a nice referral from them. You also don't know when clients' business will suddenly take off so that their business with you likewise takes off.

My philosophy is to serve everyone and keep the business at your firm. If you're too busy to deal with a particular client yourself, pass the business along to a junior person who you are confident can take care of the account. Develop an alliance with someone in your firm that you can pass smaller accounts to. Remember, profitability is in the long-term relationship.

Developing Strategic Alliances: Passing Business Along to Competitors

If, however, after careful assessment, you determine that a company is too small for you, you have options other than dumping it. One is to send the client to another smaller firm that is better suited to handle the account.

When you send clients to another firm, make sure they know that the competitor is in a much better position to serve them. You need to say something like, "We're not set up as well to serve your present needs. I checked around and found that XYZ company is better suited to serve you."

Track and measure the percentage of repeat business.

Also, make sure the competing firm knows you are sending it the business. It may want to send you business in return as a way of thanking you. In fact, you may find the best resolution is to form a strategic alliance with the smaller firm, changing it from a competitor into a partner, and regularly send it accounts that don't fit in with your business plan.

Perhaps this firm will reciprocate. In a sense, you're keeping the clients you send to your partner because you'll benefit from the goodwill of the former client and the referrals that client and your partner firm will send you.

Lastly, every once in a while you are bound to come across a client whom you do not want for life and whom you really don't want to send to a strategic partner. Some people will never be satisfied, no matter what you do, but they are rare. Here's a suggestion: Refer this client to a competitor who is not a business partner and who may be better able to serve his needs.

There are so many opportunities to have excellent lifetime clients that you shouldn't get hung up on one or two who are more trouble than they are worth.

Before you pursue new clients, maximize your relationships with your existing clients. Take the clients to whom you have made a sale and, by applying the tools offered in this book, systemizing your business and gaining client feedback, develop a partnership with them. You will build a stronger business by maximizing your existing business relationships.

Seek to forge a deeper partnership with your clients.

THINGS TO DO "MONDAY MORNING"

- **Determine what percentage of a client's business you have.** Ask clients what you can do to earn the rest of their business.
- **Determine the lifetime value of a client.** Continually share that assessment with every person in your organization.
- **When possible,** refer clients with mutual interests to each other.
- **Refer clients you can't properly serve** to junior associates or to competitors.

Expanding Your Client Base

LIFETIME TOOL

12

CUSTOMER ONCE, CLIENT FOREVER

In this chapter, I'll share:

- **Why referrals are an excellent way to develop lifetime clients**
- **How to earn referrals that expand your client base**

Most businesses don't want merely to maintain their client base but to expand it. Even if you're just trying to stay at the level of business you have now, clients are bound to leave at some point.

The most effective way to grow your business is through your existing client base. Why pursue new business when you have so much potential business in front of you? The best way to tap into this business is through referral sales.

Most businesspeople ask for referrals at all the wrong times. They either ask right after meeting someone, before they have demonstrated value, or long after a transaction or project is completed. By asking the right people for referrals at the proper time, you will catapult yourself into a new league of clients. Let's share some strategies you can begin to use today to increase your referral business.

Do Outstanding Work

Let me say right up front that the single most effective strategy to get referrals is to always do outstanding work. Ideally, you don't want to ask for referrals; you want clients to be so impressed with you that they automatically refer you to others with their highest recommendations. To achieve this, consistently exceed your clients' expectations on every transaction.

When all is said and done, you want your client to say that it has been a pleasure doing business with you.

TRUE STORY: The Value and Ease of Referrals

The best way to win referrals is to do outstanding work.

Years ago, a client recommended that I call an environmental engineering association to present a workshop. I called and sent information to the director. We spoke once or twice, but I didn't have any luck scheduling a workshop. I saw the same client about a year later. He recommended that I call the director again. Again, no luck scheduling a workshop. I can't blame the association—*I* was pursuing *it*.

Before I could arrange for a conference call with my client and director, I presented a workshop to another environmental engineering company. In the audience was one of the association's board members. I guess he enjoyed the workshop because he called me a couple of weeks later and asked me for a proposal for not one but two workshops for the association. He clearly laid out the requirements of each workshop and the budget. I faxed him the proposal.

A week later the director called me, approved the proposal, booked the dates for the workshops and asked me when I wanted to pick up the deposit check. No fuss, no muss.

The moral of this story is: Do outstanding work and your clients will pursue *you*. The sale and the lifetime relationship are a lot easier when clients are calling you.

As I pointed out, when you do it right, referrals are the by-products of excellent service. Referrals cost you absolutely nothing. You can spend time, effort and money on advertising, or you can perform excellent work and receive leads and sales through referrals. The choice is yours.

I've included a letter on page 252 from Dennis Clarken, who attended a GoalStar workshop and found great benefit in pursuing referrals. I include this letter not because of Dennis's kind words about my workshop but because of his success at practicing the strategies. As he says, "It's all there for the asking!"

First demonstrate value, then ask, "Who else may we serve?"

QUESTIONS FOR YOU

- *In your clients' eyes, are you performing outstanding work?*
- *How do you know?*
- *Would your current clients say you are a pleasure to do business with?*

Always Ask for Referrals

The second-best strategy for getting referrals is to ask for them—a simple strategy most businesspeople forget. No matter where you work in a company, you can always ask clients, "Who else can we serve?"

The best time to ask for a referral or testimonial is after you've demonstrated excellent value to a client: when a client gushes over you and tells you how happy he is with your service. Then you might say, "Thank you so much for the kind words. Could you put that in writing, and is there anyone else we can serve?" You gain two things: You plant the seed for future business, and you get a nice letter to share with prospective clients.

Don't ask any client for a referral or testimo-

"IT'S ALL THERE FOR THE ASKING!"

DANAHER INSURANCE

June 23, 1998

Mr. Richard Buckingham
GoalStar Business Strategies, Inc.
4813 St. Elmo Avenue
Bethesda, MD 20814

Dear Rick:

Thank you for the information and your note. I am feeling much better thanks. I wanted to share a little story with you.

I believe that any piece of information that you obtain from these meetings can be helpful. Even though I had to leave early I did get something from our time together. While I was out sick I reviewed my goals and added a few. One was to ask for 3 referrals from all of my customers at renewal and get back in the habit of using testimonial letters.

One of my better customers owns a large crematorium and deals with most of the funeral homes in the area. When I went to review coverages with him I brought along a testimonial for him to copy onto letterhead and sign. He teased me a little for "writing my own ticket", but he did sign it. Than he asked his daughter (the office manager) to print out his client list. I now have a list of over 50 funeral homes to call on with his blessing and HE suggested that I send HIS letter out to them prior to setting appointments.

It is all there for the asking!!!

Sincerely,

D.C.

Dennis P. Clarken

DPC/89249

Thomas P. Danaher & Company, Inc. 4200 Evergreen Lane, Annandale, Virginia 22003 • 703-642-3200 • FAX 703-642-5970 nial letter on your first appointment or before you have delivered your product or service. You need to prove yourself first and establish a relationship of trust. Nobody wants to recommend a friend or associate to a firm when the work is unproven or not of the highest quality.

Lastly, when you ask, do not use the word "referral." Say instead, "Who else can we serve?" Remember, business is all about serving others.

Clients are easier to win when they initiate the call.

TRUE STORY: How and When to Ask for Referrals

I was recently at the bank with a client, an attorney named George, when one of his clients came in. George's client raved, and I mean raved, about George's performance. The client liked both George's service and George's personality, and told him what a pleasure it was to do business with him. George just blushed and thanked him.

After his client left, I suggested to George that the next time he should thank the client for his kind words, and then do two other things. First, he should ask his client to put his compliments in writing, so George can include this letter in all future proposals. Second, right after the client gushed about his service, George should have asked the magical question: "That is nice of you to say. Who else may I serve?" Even if your client doesn't have anyone immediately in mind, at least you plant the seed for future referrals.

Most businesspeople, if they ask for referrals at all, ask at the wrong time, either too soon in the relationship or too late, when it's awkward. The best time to ask for a referral is immediately after a client has praised your service.

QUESTIONS FOR YOU

- *When was the last time you asked a client, "Who else may we serve?"*
- *What three people will you call today and ask, "Who else may we serve?"*

Learn as much as you can about new clients before you call them.

Learn About Prospective Clients

When you get a referral, set yourself up to win by learning as much as you can about your referral client before you make initial contact. Go to the referral clients' Web site. Absorb as much information as you can. Find common ground between you and the client before you meet. The chapter on building rapport (Lifetime Tool 5) has strategies you can use to find common ground.

Find out about referral clients' previous buying habits, loyalties and relationships. Whom have they done business with? How did it go? Are they difficult to please? Why are they looking for someone new? Anything you can learn about prospective clients before you talk to them is extremely helpful. The more prepared you are, the better your chances of winning a sale and developing a lifetime relationship.

In addition, you want to protect yourself. In doing this due diligence, you might find out that certain clients are more trouble than they are worth. If, in fact, you do find out something negative about your referral, don't immediately dismiss the referral outright. Meet with the client, draw him or her out, and attempt to verify the information you have heard.

Give Qualified Referrals to Get Referrals

One of the best ways to get referrals is to give referrals for qualified people. I stress the word "qualified" because you want to refer only qualified people. One of the quickest and surest ways to squash any business relationship is to refer someone who is not qualified. Then you lose all credibility with a client.

Refer one qualified client to another client today.

QUESTION FOR YOU

- *What clients can you call today to refer to other clients or associates?*

Build Bridges in Giving Referrals

When you give clients or associates referrals, set everyone up to win by warming up the client to the firm whom you are referring. Don't just give clients the name and telephone number of someone to call. Tell each party—both the client you are giving the referral to and the person you are referring—about each other. Help them find common ground. Perhaps set up a conference call to introduce them to each other.

Better yet, when appropriate, set up a lunch or some other activity, such as a golf outing, with your associate and the referral source. Be generous to both parties in making introductions in person—say something good about each one. Remember, you are providing value to both parties.

When you receive a referral, have your referral source set you up to win by doing the same.

Keep Your Referral Sources in the Loop and Thank Them for the Business

Remember to keep your referral sources in the loop during the sales process. Enlist their support when you need it. When you reach an impasse with a prospective client, remember that you have a resource that you can turn to for advice and guidance.

Immediately and properly thank people for their referrals.

After you have finalized the sale, the very next call you should make is to your referral source thanking him for the business. By making this telephone call you are not only being polite and gracious, you are also greatly increasing your chances of getting future referrals.

At the least, you owe your referral source a telephone call. Better yet, be creative, and think of an appropriate gift for your referral source. The better you know your referral source, the more appropriate your gift will be. The more generous and appropriate the gift, the greater the possibility of additional referrals.

TRUE STORY: A Thank-You Plants the Seeds for More Referrals

Gerry Ryan is the general sales manager of a local Chevrolet dealership. I once sent one of my clients to Gerry to buy a van. I was out of town when my client purchased the van from Gerry. The first day I was back in my office, Gerry called to thank me for the referral. He had called earlier, he said, reached my voice mail and decided that rather than leave a message, he would call later to thank me in person—a nice touch that impressed me with his genuine gratitude.

QUESTIONS FOR YOU

- *Do you think I will refer more clients to Gerry?*
- *Are you properly thanking people for their referrals?*

Measure Referrals

Ask your best client; get the best referral.

At the beginning of this book, when we discussed how to continually improve (Lifetime Tool 1), I suggested that when you want to improve any behavior, you should measure it. Here is an excellent opportunity to do just that. How much of last month's or last year's sales were the result of referrals? What percentage of your referrals result in successful deals?

I recently met with the head of training for a large national financial institution. He told me he wanted to increase his firm's referral business. My immediate response was to ask what the current percentage of referral business was. He told me his firm had not been measuring it.

How can you improve unless you are measuring your performance? When you want to improve any behavior, measure it.

Besides maximizing your existing clients, referral sales are the easiest strategy for growing your business. Referrals should be the by-product of doing excellent work. The last strategy in developing lifetime clients is to gain the referrals that you have worked hard to earn. In short, reap what you have sown.

(continued)

THINGS TO DO "MONDAY MORNING"

- **Always do outstanding work.** Earn referrals.
- **After a client praises your service,** always ask, "Who else may we serve?"
- **When possible and appropriate,** give business to you clients.
- **To make the most of referrals,** completely research prospective clients before you contact them.
- **Track and measure the percentage** of referral business.

Today Is "Monday Morning"

MONDAY MORNING

CUSTOMER ONCE, CLIENT FOREVER

"Talking doesn't bring the wood in."
—IRISH SAYING

When I give workshops I usually receive a range of feedback. Out of 100 feedback forms, I receive one or two that, in a terse sentence or two, say something like, "A lot of ideas I already know."

I am always grateful to receive feedback from anyone, so it's with extreme gratitude that I want to ask these people, "Great! Now what will you do today to apply these ideas?"

If you've heard these strategies before, the question now is, "Are you applying them to the best of your ability?" Long-term success will occur with the constant application of these strategies. You have taken your time to read this book, you have invested your money—now go out and reap your rewards. You may have heard some of these ideas before, and some may be new to you. I am suggesting you tie them together and apply them consistently.

Maybe Tim Miller, a vice-president with a large financial-services company, summed it up best. After an evening workshop, he told his people: "It is not what we covered tonight that matters; it is what you do with it Monday morning that ultimately matters."

Today entirely too much emphasis is placed on speakers and trainers—the messengers—rather than on what they have to say—the message. Messengers tend to have clay feet. Therefore, you need to focus on the message. The tools I've described here won't do you any good at all unless you work hard at implementing them.

I toyed with the idea of including a final tool—"Working Hard." All the bright ideas in the world won't help you if you don't work hard at implementing them. Hard work is the key to succeeding. You must work hard by:

Long-term business success comes with constant application of these strategies.

- **Constantly looking inward and seeking ways to continually improve**
- **Recognizing and acknowledging your own perceived shortcomings and correcting them**
- **Properly preparing yourself to serve your clients**
- **Consistently serving and superserving clients**
- **Building the proper rapport with your clients**
- **Listening effectively to clients**
- **Taking the time to ask clients better questions, soliciting their input and implementing their suggestions**
- **Systemizing your business**
- **Turning complaining clients into lifetime clients**
- **Maintaining the loyalty of the clients you have and attracting new ones**

All of this is hard work—but rewarding. As promised, when you use all of the tools in this guide, you will not only gain lifetime clients, you will find greater joy and satisfaction in your work.

My greatest hope is that after reading this book you will look at your work and see all the new opportunities for getting closer to your clients. I hope you recognize the opportunity for success that lies in repeat and referral business, and that ultimate success is in the lifetime client relationship.

Today is Monday morning! Start using the tools in this book immediately to start improving your performance. And don't stop there. Read other books, listen to your associates and clients, take training seminars—do whatever you can to continue to improve. It's an ongoing process.

Following this chapter is a final lifetime tool, a list of books you can start with. I have read all these books and found helpful information in all of them. I hope you find them helpful, too.

In closing, let me offer one final suggestion: Just pick one client and apply all these strategies. From your first encounter, position yourself as the trusted adviser, call the client before he calls you, sharpen your listening skills, ask better questions, deliver outstanding service, and solicit feedback. Notice the results. See how much additional business the client freely gives you. Track the referral business from this client. Notice how you feel dealing with the client. When you feel the success, apply all these strategies to other clients.

Soon you will see just how valuable and rewarding lifetime clients can be to your career.

Best wishes!

Books That Have Helped Me

If you have any trouble locating these books or wish to recommend a book, please call 301-913-0222, or e-mail me at rdb@goalstar.com. (*Please note that books marked with an asterisk are religious in nature.)

Leadership

BENNIS, WARREN G. *On Becoming a Leader.* Reading, Mass.: Addison Wesley Longman, 1994.

BENNIS, WARREN G. AND BIEDERMAN, PATRICIA WARD. *Organizing Genius: The Secrets of Creative Collaboration.* New Jersey: Harper Collins, 1998.

I enjoy Warren Bennis's books. Both these books are helpful in gaining a greater appreciation of everyday leadership. In *Organizing Genius,* Bennis and Biederman study and share real-life leadership examples from many different fields: science, politics, education and even show business.

COLLINS, JAMES C. AND PORRAS, JERRY I. *Built to Last: Successful Habits of Visionary Companies.* New York: Harper Business, 1994.

An outstanding study of companies that have enjoyed long-term business success compared with competitors who have not enjoyed the same level of success. This book includes a wealth of information and is excellent for managers, owners and CEOs.

DEMING, W. EDWARDS. *Out of the Crisis: Quality, Productivity and Competitive Position.* Cambridge, New York: Cambridge University Press, 1988.

Deming's book might be difficult to locate and read, but the two books about him and his business philosophy, by Andrea Gabor (below) and Mary Walton (page 266), are excellent.

ELLIS, JOSEPH. *Passionate Sage: The Character and Legacy of John Adams.* New York: W.W. Norton & Co., 1993.

A good historical portrait of a committed president who was more concerned with America's long-term success than his own popularity.

GABOR, ANDREA. *The Man Who Discovered Quality: How W. Edwards Deming Brought Quality to America: The Stories of Ford, Xerox and GM.* New York Times Books, 1990.
See Deming above.

GOODWIN, DORIS KEARNS. *No Ordinary Time: Franklin and Eleanor Roosevelt: The Home Front in World War II.* New York: Simon and Schuster, 1994.

A great book on leadership with many outstanding leadership examples. Goodwin makes you feel as if you are at the White House with Franklin and Eleanor Roosevelt during World War II. If you are a business leader, read especially the chapter, "By God, If It Isn't Old Frank!" Like him or loathe him, Roosevelt was able to mobilize an initially reluctant country behind the war effort, and presided over one of the largest and most successful military buildups ever. As a result, the Allied forces, with far fewer years of preparation, were able to defeat the Axis powers.

JONES, LAURIE BETH. *Jesus CEO: Using Ancient Wisdom for Visionary Leadership*. New York, Hyperion, 1995.*

KATZENBACH, JON AND SMITH, DOUGLAS K. *The Wisdom of Teams*. New York: Harper Business, 1994.

Probably the best book on team building I have read, this well-researched book studies a variety of teams.

KOTTER, JOHN P. *Leading Change*. Boston: Harvard Business School Press, 1996.

LOWENSTEIN, ROGER. *Buffett: The Making of an American Capitalist*. New York: Random House, 1995.

MARANISS, DAVID. *When Pride Still Mattered: A Life of Vince Lombardi*. New York: Simon & Schuster, 1999.

An excellent book that details how Vince Lombardi was able to turn around a losing football franchise, the Green Bay Packers, and win five national championships in nine years. In essence, Lombardi took a group of ordinary individuals and turned them into an extraordinary team. The book doesn't mention this, but an inordinate number of Lombardi players also became millionaires, and they credit Lombardi's coaching for their business success.

MARRIOTT, J. WILLARD AND BROWN, KATHI ANNE. *The Spirit to Serve.* New York: Harper Business, 1997.

A must read; 200 pages you will read in a night or two. Marriott clearly explains why Marriott is successful. You will find chapters on listening as well as the importance of business systems. The title itself is worth the price of the book. At the time this book was going to press, I was informed that *The Spirit to Serve* was out of print but available at Marriott Hotels. It's well worth tracking down.

PHILLIPS, DONALD T. *Lincoln on Leadership: Executive Strategies for Tough Times.* New York: Warner Books, 1992.

SIDEY, HUGH. *John F. Kennedy, President.* New York: Atheneum, 1963.

Out of print, but well worth tracking down. Like Goodwin's book, many excellent examples of leadership, especially President Kennedy's response after the Bay of Pigs.

SLATER, ROBERT. *Get Better or Get Beaten: 31 Leadership Strategies From GE's Jack Welch.* Burr Ridge, Ill.: Irwin Professional Pub., 1994.

WALTON, MARY. *Deming Management at Work.* New York: Perigree Books, 1991.
See Deming on page 264.

Production/Business Management

GOLDRATT, ELIYAHU M. AND COX, HEFF. *The Goal: A Process of Ongoing Improvement.* Great

Barrington, MA: North River Press, 1992.

A fictionalized account of a manager trying to turn around a declining factory. I won't tell you the result. Many practical examples of how to improve an organization.

LOVE, JOHN F. *McDonald's Behind the Arches.* New York: Bantam Books, 1986.

This must-read book chronicles why McDonald's was successful through 1986. Just as McDonald's is meticulous about the preparation of its food, the author goes to great lengths to explain McDonald's success. For example, Love details all of McDonald's research to develop the perfect French fry. If you like Lifetime Tool 8, Systemizing Your Business, you will enjoy this book. Especially important for managers and owners.

WALTON, SAM AND HUEY, JOHN. *Sam Walton: Made in America.* New York, Doubleday, 1993.

Another must-read. Not only a great rags-to-riches story, but a book filled with many outstanding business strategies. In many ways, Walton was a business revolutionary.

YATES, BROCK. The Critical Path. Boston: Little, Brown and Co., 1996.

Personal Development

ALBOM, MITCH. *Tuesdays with Morrie.* New York: Doubleday, 1997.

ASHE, ARTHUR AND RAMPERSAD, ARNOLD. *Days of Grace: A Memoir.* New York: Alfred A. Knopf, 1993.

A wonderful book by a humble and gentle man. Ashe says he tried to live his life by the philosophy that he wouldn't do something during the day that he couldn't tell his mother at the end of the day. It may sound hokey, but it's not a bad way to live.

CARNEGIE, DALE. *How to Stop Worrying and Start Living.* New York: Simon and Schuster, 1984.

COVEY, STEPHEN. *The Seven Habits of Highly Effective People.* Thorndike, Me.: G. K. Hall, 1997.

FOX, EMMET. *Sermon on the Mount: The Key to Success in Life.* San Francisco: Harper & Row, 1989.*

FRANKL, VIKTOR E. *Man's Search for Meaning.* Boston: Beacon Press, 1992.

A short and powerful account of Frankl's time in a Nazi concentration camp during World War II.

HILL, NAPOLEON. *Think and Grow Rich.* New York: Hawthorn Books, 1966.

JEFFERS, SUSAN. *Feel the Fear and Do It Anyway.* San Diego: Harcourt Brace Jovanovich, 1987.

If you procrastinate or are stuck in your life, you must read this book. I gave it to a friend who wanted to start her own business and was hesitating. After reading the book, she started her business. Her sales the first year were double her projections!

KING, MARTIN LUTHER. *Strength to Love.* New York: Harper & Row, 1963.*

A collection of excellent sermons a young King preached during the Montgomery Bus

Boycott in the 1950s. I have read and reread these sermons numerous times and found great inspiration. Read this book to learn how King conducted a national struggle for equal rights on the "high plains of human dignity and discipline."

MOTHER TERESA. *The Simple Path.* New York: Ballantine Books, 1995.*

PEALE, NORMAN VINCENT. *The Power of Positive Thinking.* New York: Prentice Hall Press, 1987.*

PECK, M. SCOTT. *The Road Less Traveled.* New York: Simon and Schuster, 1985.

PRICE, REYNOLDS. *Letter to a Man in the Fire: Does God Exist and Does He Care?* New York: Scribner, 1999.*

An interesting book by a Duke English professor written in response to a letter from a young man dying of cancer. Price is a brilliant man who draws on many religious sources in trying to answer the question of God's existence. The best parts of the book are when Price speaks of his own struggles with cancer.

ROBBINS, ANTHONY. *Awaken the Giant Within: How to Take Immediate Control of Your Mental, Emotional, Physical and Financial Destiny.* New York: Summit Books, 1991.

—*Unlimited Power: The New Science of Personal Achievement.* New York: Simon and Schuster, 1997.

STALLINGS, GENE AND COOK, SALLY. *Another Season: A Coach's Story of Raising an Exceptional*

Son. Boston: Little Brown and Co., 1997.

STEINEM, GLORIA. *Revolution From Within: A Book of Self-Esteem.* Boston: Little Brown and Co., 1992.

A wonderful book on self-esteem. I bought this book to better understand women and ended up learning more about myself. You will be more successful in business and life when you better understand yourself. The Buddhist inscription in the beginning of the book is priceless: "You've come here to find what you already have." Wonder why the first chapter of my book focuses on you and continual improvement?

Successful Selling

BECKER, HAL WITH FLORENCE MUSTRIC. *Can I Have 5 Minutes of Your Time?* Cleveland, Ohio: Oakhill Press, 1993.

CARNEGIE, DALE. *How to Win Friends and Influence People.* New York: Pocket Books, 1982.

The granddaddy of business-relationship books, a must-read. When you want to improve your relationships, business and otherwise, read this book. What Carnegie suggested in the 1930s is just as applicable today.

CATES, BILL. *Unlimited Referrals: Secrets That Turn Business Relationships to Gold.* Wheaton, Md.: Thunder Hill Press, 1996.

DELMAR, KEN. *Winning Moves: The Body Language of Selling.* New York: Warner Books, 1984.

A wonderful book on the importance of body language, and fun, too.

GIRARD, JOE AND SHOOK, ROBERT. *How to Close Every Sale.* New York: Warner Books, 1989.

MACKAY, HARVEY. *Swim with the Sharks Without Being Eaten Alive: Outsell, Outmanage, Outmotivate, Outnegotiate Your Competition.* New York: Morrow, 1988.

Short chapters filled with great business and personal strategies. Read especially the "Mackay 66." Mackay eats, drinks and sleeps business.

MORGAN, EDMUND S. *The Genius of George Washington.* New York: W.W. Norton & Co., 1980.

A short book that strips away the myth of Washington and exposes his true genius. Washington recognized that the best alliances are those in which everyone wins. He constantly thought about what's in it for the other party. If Washington were alive today, he could be a great businessman.

Excellent Customer Service

CONELLAN, THOMAS K., AND ZEMKE, RON. *Sustaining Knocking Your Socks Off Customer Service.* New York: Amacom, 1993.

DONNELLY, JAMES H., JR., *Close to the Customer.* Homewood, IL: Business One Irwin, 1992.

GROSS, T. SCOTT. *Positively Outrageous Service.* New York: Warner Books, 1991.

LISWOOD, LAURA A. *Serving Them Right.* New York: Harper Business, 1991.

RECK, ROSS R. *Turn Your Customers Into Your Sales Force: The Art of Winning Repeat and Referral Customers.* New York: Prentice Hall, 1991.

SEWELL, CARL AND BROWN, PAUL B. *Customers for Life.* New York: Pocket Books, 1990.

Another must-read, this outstanding business book is perhaps the best on this list. Anyone in business will benefit by the great business strategies shared in this book.

Index

C

U

V

W

Survey

GOALSTAR CONTINUAL IMPROVEMENT SURVEY

Thank you for reading *Customer Once, Client Forever* and filling out this survey. You can fax this survey to 301-913-0223, e-mail it to rdb@goalstar.com, or fill out a blank form at www.goalstar.com. (All five of the following items are optional.)

Name and title:______________________________

Company:______________________________

Telephone:______________________________

E-mail:______________________________

What major strategies did you learn and will you implement from reading this book?

1. ______________________________
2. ______________________________
3. ______________________________
4. ______________________________
5. ______________________________
6. ______________________________
7. ______________________________
8. ______________________________
9. ______________________________
10. ______________________________
11. ______________________________
12. ______________________________

(continued)

GOALSTAR CONTINUAL IMPROVEMENT SURVEY

Did *Customer Once, Client Forever* meet or exceed your expectations? Why or why not?

____

____

____

On a scale of 1 to 10, with 10 being the best, how do you rate *Customer Once, Client Forever*? If you didn't give it a 10, what specifically can I do to make it a 10?

____

____

____

Which chapters did you enjoy the most?

____

____

____

Which chapters need "continual improvement"?

____

____

____

Did I miss any topics that I should have covered? What topics can I address to make you more successful? (Please include your name and address so that I might send any pertinent articles.)

____

____

____

About the Author

Exhilarating. Captivating. Eye-opening. Best presentation yet. This is just some of the praise Richard Buckingham has received from his listeners—and this for someone who was once terrified of public speaking. Mr. Buckingham took his own advice (Lifetime Tool 1: Continually Improve Yourself), educated himself as a speaker, and is now president of GoalStar Business Strategies, a training and consulting company located in Bethesda, Md.

Mr. Buckingham speaks nationally to share skills and strategies with businesspeople and organizations who want to achieve:

- **Lifetime clients**
- **Excellent customer service**
- **Profitable business management**
- **Leadership and team building**

He conducts workshops and provides consulting services for a variety of industries, including real estate, insurance, public relations, management consulting, financial services, automotive, construction, law, franchising, accounting, and information technology. Mr. Buckingham's clients include Fortune 100 companies and closely held concerns. Major corporate clients include: Bank of America, Merrill Lynch, American Express Financial Advisors, AT&T Wireless, YEO, Monumental Life Insurance Co., CarrAmerica

Real Estate Services and USAA Realty. Clients universally praise the practical value and enthusiasm of Mr. Buckingham's presentations.

Earlier in his career, Mr. Buckingham sold and managed projects for more than 15 years in the commercial construction industry.

Besides writing *Customer Once, Client Forever,* Mr. Buckingham has written numerous articles on sales, customer service and business management. They have appeared in publications such as the *Washington Business Journal* and *Personal Selling Power* magazine, and he has been quoted in the *Washington Post,* the *Washington Business Journal* and *Investor's Business Daily.*

Mr. Buckingham is a graduate of Yale University and lives in Bethesda, Md.

Contact information. If you enjoyed this book and are interested in retaining Mr. Buckingham's services, you may reach him one of the following ways:

- **301-913-0222 telephone**
- **301-913-0223 fax**
- **e-mail: rdb@goalstar.com**
- **Web site: www.goalstar.com**

Services. Mr. Buckingham's services include:

- **Business assessments**
- **Consulting services in the area of sales, customer service, business management, and associate development and retention**
- **Developing corporate training programs**
- **Client focus groups**

Training programs. Mr. Buckingham's current training programs include:

- Lifetime Tools, Lifetime Clients
- Consistently Exceeding Client Expectations
- Profitable Project/Business Management
- Leadership and Team Building
- Maximizing Your Associates' Contributions
- Achieving Business Excellence